QUANTUM
LEADERSHIP

QUANTUM
LEADERSHIP

Igniting the limitless
power of people
in disruptive times

Rob Balmer

Published in 2021 by Robert Balmer

Robert Balmer
151 Pullenvale Road
Pullenvale
Queensland 4069
0425 247 156

A catalogue record for this work is available from the National Library of Australia

ISBN 978-0-646-82913-5

Edited by Sophie Church, HistorySmiths
Designed by Lexi Johnstone, Lexi Ink Design & Print

Contents

Introduction

We live in a world that is changing ever more quickly, where social and technological disruptions are everywhere, where innovations can change entire industries at a frighteningly rapid rate, where IT and telecommunications have created a 24/7 'never off' work environment, and where the 'instant gratification' expectations of many stakeholders create pressure for rapid outcomes. It is my contention that modern organisational leaders need to evolve their leadership approaches to better cater to this environment.

Don't panic! I am not proposing to discard all the great theories and models of leadership that have been espoused. They still have their place and are still very relevant. Many of the leadership theories I have been exposed to over the years certainly deliver great results, particularly when they are applied properly and in a sustained way. However, they tend to drive slower, more gradual, more incremental changes to performance and culture in organisations. They are a bit like a changing tide — slow and steady, but the difference between high and low tide can be quite significant. If leaders can create a constant and positive tidal flow in the performance and cultures of their organisations, this is still definitely highly desirable.

I believe, though, that leaders of modern organisations need to add a new approach to their arsenal of leadership skills. They need to be able to drive much faster, more radical changes to performance and culture when they find themselves and their organisations operating in more volatile environments. Such environments will become increasingly normal as we move into the third decade of the twenty-first century. In fact, most organisations are already operating in unpredictable contexts most of the time, even though they may not realise it. Instead of a constant and positive tidal flow, the impact leaders need to create is more like that of a wormhole through space-time, where huge distances can be traversed, and massive changes can occur almost in an instant!

At the time of writing, in mid-2020, the world is in the grip of the Covid-19 pandemic, undoubtedly the biggest sustained global disruption since World War Two. The pandemic and the resulting restrictions and lockdowns have affected every aspect of our lives and forced us all to make changes in the way we live. The crisis has also forced almost every organisation to significantly change the way in which it works and can continue to operate sustainably. Sadly, many organisations will not survive. Those that do will be permanently changed.

While it is easy to view the Covid-19 pandemic as a one-off, out-of-the-blue situation, my view is that it is just a magnified example of the kinds of disruptions that have been happening all around organisations for at least the last 20 years. To be reminded of the global challenges we have already faced this century, it is necessary only to think of events such as 9/11 and the global financial crisis (GFC), and the periods of political and economic instability that followed. In the commercial domain, the expanding list of world-leading organisations that have either ceased to exist, or have had their positions of dominance dramatically weakened, is further evidence of this disruption.

The truth is that the rate of change and disruption will never again be as slow as it is today. It will only continue to accelerate, pushed by factors in our society that are themselves evolving exponentially. Organisations need to become much more 'fit for change' and their leaders need to adapt their leadership approaches to be equally 'fit for change'. Leaders must be able to create positive, adaptive cultures where people can not only survive change, but thrive in it.

Over the last 30 years, I have been led through major changes by some wonderful corporate leaders, from whom I learned many lessons. I was also very fortunate to be able to lead the large and rapidly growing consumer business of Compaq Computer Australia through the explosive growth and volatile market conditions of the 1990s. Since 2004, I have had the honour of leading Executive Central, a company I co-founded, in which capacity I have worked with hundreds of executives and emerging leaders, each attempting to deal with the challenges and opportunities of their own organisations and careers. These experiences, including the many mistakes I have made or experienced others making, have brought me to the point where I feel the time is right to challenge many traditional conventions about organisational leadership.

This book equips leaders with a new approach to leadership that can be applied at an individual, team, or organisation-wide level and which can produce rapid, positive outcomes in response to rapid change. I share new ways of applying strategies that have proven to be successful both in my own corporate leadership career and for the clients with whom I have had the privilege to work over the last 20 years as an executive coach. I also introduce new strategies that will enhance any leader's capabilities to make a quantum leap in their own leadership skills, enabling them to be better prepared to rise to the challenges of the dynamic, exciting and unpredictable organisational environments that are our new normal.

To further enhance the value that I hope you will take from your reading, I have included QR codes throughout this book which link to additional video content on the topic under discussion. All you need to do is hover your phone or tablet's camera over the QR code and you will be provided with a link to the relevant video. I hope you enjoy the additional insights these videos provide.

CHAPTER 1

Quantum leadership explained

What is quantum leadership? In short, it is leadership that 'excites' a quantum leap in the performance of individuals, teams, or entire organisations. It is leadership that produces an instantaneous positive change in performance at any one of these levels, as opposed to a longer-term gradual change in performance. It is leadership that is appropriate for environments where rapid change and disruption is significantly impacting on the status quo of an organisation — I call these 'quantum environments'.

The quantum physics metaphor

One of the foundational principles of quantum physics involves the behaviour of quantum particles, such as electrons and photons. These do not behave in the same manner as other particles or objects. The normal rules of physics do not accurately describe quantum particle behaviour. Quantum physics is an entirely different discipline that was developed to try to understand particle behaviour at the sub-atomic level.

I would like to focus specifically on the concept of the 'quantum leap'. Basically, each quantum particle can exist at a number of very specific energy levels, known as quantum levels, and nowhere in between. If energy is introduced to a quantum particle at one of the quantum levels, that energy excites a 'quantum leap' and the particle ceases to exist at the old quantum level, and instantaneously begins existing at a different quantum level.

The "quantum" realm
How quantum particles behave

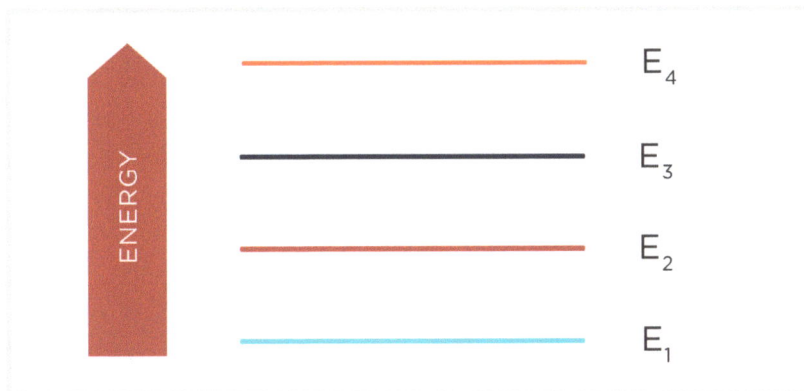

Quantum particles (e.g. electrons) only exist at certain energy levels - and nowhere in between!

When energy is introduced to a quantum particle, a 'quantum leap' occurs and the particle stops existing at one state and instantly exists at a different state.

- There is no evidence of movement or acceleration of the particle, it is an *instant change* from one state to another

This is where quantum physics gets really interesting. When a particle makes a quantum leap, its movement from one energy state to another cannot be measured. There is no acceleration, velocity, momentum, inertia or any of the characteristics of movement that are normally observed when objects or particles move from one place to another. The quantum leap is instantaneous and significant. The quantum particle simply disappears from one quantum level and instantaneously re-appears at another. This begs the question, where does the particle go in between levels? The concept of parallel dimensions or universes was born from the quantum leap — the particle must go somewhere, mustn't it?

Let's bring the concept back into the world of leadership and organisational performance. I firmly believe that individuals, teams and organisations — let's call these 'entities' — are just like quantum particles in that they tend to exist at any one of a number of defined energy or quantum levels. I will explore this concept further shortly. Quantum leadership means using leadership as the energy to excite a quantum leap to higher states of being in any entity, which results in a sudden significant increase or advance in performance. It is this kind of increase or advance that is required if organisations are to survive and thrive in quantum environments.

Individual quantum levels

There are many ways to define the states at which individuals exist at any one time, but let's use a model that has been at the heart of modern psychology, Maslow's hierarchy of needs. Abraham Maslow identified a number of psychological 'states of being' in individuals. The following diagram provides a good summary of these states. I have modified the descriptions of each state to apply them to the context of individuals working in organisations.

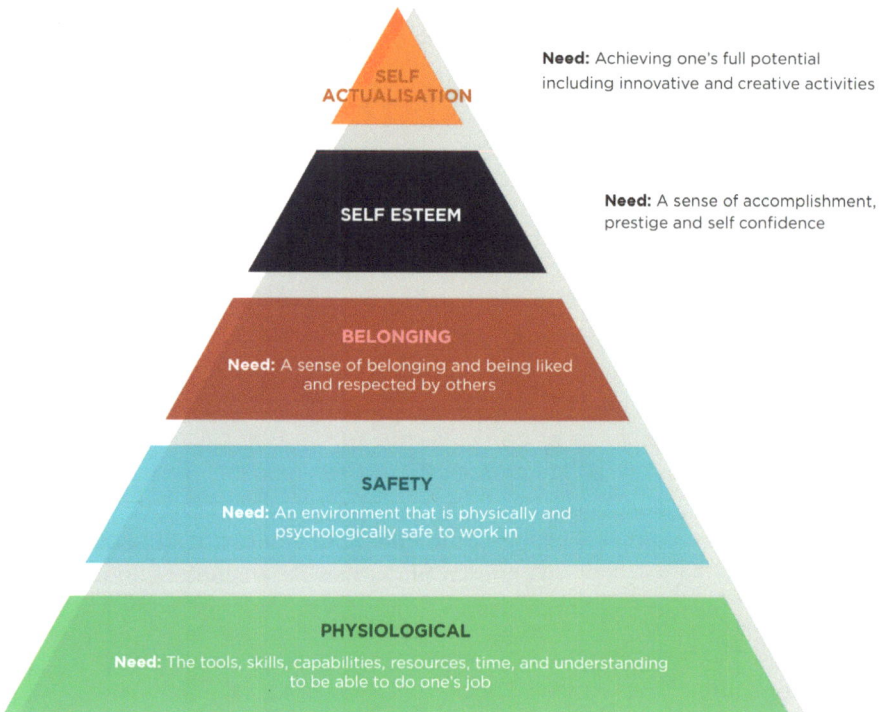

SELF ACTUALISATION
Need: Achieving one's full potential including innovative and creative activities

SELF ESTEEM
Need: A sense of accomplishment, prestige and self confidence

BELONGING
Need: A sense of belonging and being liked and respected by others

SAFETY
Need: An environment that is physically and psychologically safe to work in

PHYSIOLOGICAL
Need: The tools, skills, capabilities, resources, time, and understanding to be able to do one's job

The quantum level at which an individual exists within an organisation is the level below that at which their needs are not being met. Individual quantum levels can be described as follows:

Physiological — Individuals have the basic tools, skills, resources, time and understanding to be able to do their jobs. As such, they feel they have the capability to perform their roles. If these needs are not being met, individuals feel a constant sense of inadequacy and fear that they will not survive in the organisation for long.

Safety — Individuals feel physically or psychologically safe in their work environments. As such, they add a degree of trust to their basic level of capability to perform their roles. If these needs are not being met and individuals feel some sense of threat from which they need to protect themselves, they are likely to employ defensive behaviours (which may be passive or aggressive) in the workplace.

Belonging — Individuals feel like they belong and/or are respected within their work environments. As such, they feel more motivated and energised to put in extra effort in their roles. If these needs are not being met, individuals are likely to focus their energy on getting the attention of stakeholders and convincing those people of their worth.

Self-esteem — Individuals have high self-confidence and a sense that they are accomplishing tasks successfully in their roles. They feel empowered to extend their capabilities, trusted by others, and energised to try new things. If these needs are not being met, individuals are likely to be concerned about how others perceive them and are less likely to take the opportunity to participate in challenging or prestigious opportunities and activities.

Self-actualisation — Individuals are totally at ease with who they are and are truly interested in reaching their full potential in their roles and careers. As such, they feel capable, trusted and energised to truly unlock their full potential and comfortable with the risk that comes from being truly innovative. If these needs are not being met, individuals will not be comfortable to be vulnerable with others, will take fewer risks, and will be less likely to bring all the power sources they have to contribute positively to their roles, teams and organisations.

In the context of individuals, quantum leadership is about the excitation of a sudden and significant leap from wherever each individual is currently sitting in this hierarchy of needs to a higher state of being.

Team quantum levels

My Executive Central colleagues and I have had the privilege of working with hundreds of teams over the years. We have observed that teams also exist on different quantum levels at different times, depending on the make-up of team members, the environment each team is operating in, and the type of leadership each team is receiving.

The following diagram summarises the different quantum levels of teams:

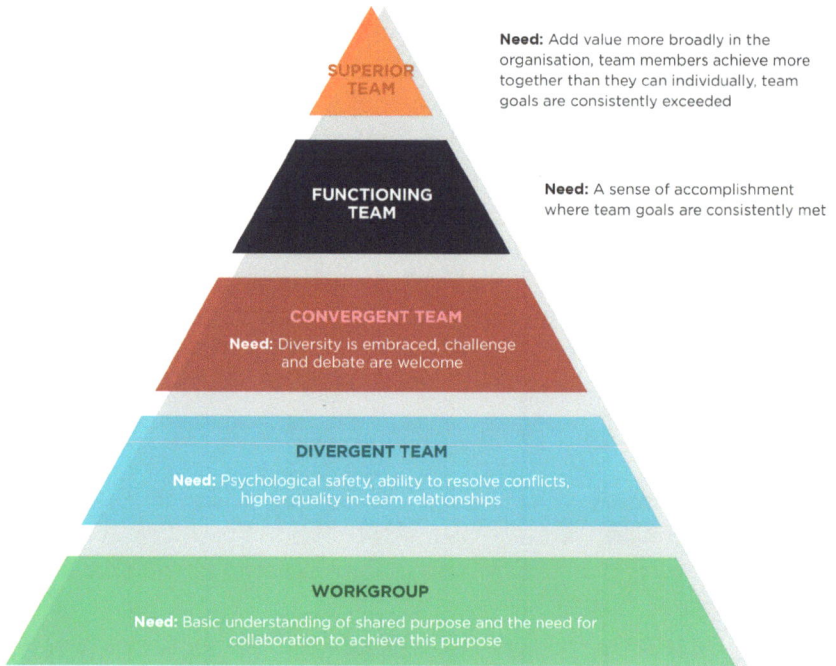

SUPERIOR TEAM

Need: Add value more broadly in the organisation, team members achieve more together than they can individually, team goals are consistently exceeded

FUNCTIONING TEAM

Need: A sense of accomplishment where team goals are consistently met

CONVERGENT TEAM
Need: Diversity is embraced, challenge and debate are welcome

DIVERGENT TEAM
Need: Psychological safety, ability to resolve conflicts, higher quality in-team relationships

WORKGROUP
Need: Basic understanding of shared purpose and the need for collaboration to achieve this purpose

The quantum level of a team's performance is the level below that at which its needs are not being met. Team quantum levels can be described as follows:

Workgroup — The team is really more of a group of individuals working independently, their only commonality being that they happen to report to the same manager. As a result, the team totally relies on the manager to allocate work tasks and to make any attempt to pull the work together into something that is co-ordinated. Team members rarely display any teaming capabilities, have transactional relationships with each other, and are not energised to do anything more than what their manager tells them to do.

Divergent team — The team does have a sense of shared purpose and team members do rely on each other's performance to achieve team goals. However, the team's performance is adversely affected by one or more issues which can include relationship conflicts, process difficulties, lack of role clarity, and lack of understanding of the shared purpose. As a result, the team will tend to have factions where team members gravitate to one side of the issue or the other and set themselves up in conflict with each other. Trust is low between team members and energy is wasted in dealing with the unresolved team issues.

Convergent team — The team has a shared purpose and generally team members get on well together. Often, a sizeable number of team members will have worked together for an extended period and have strong relationships and interpersonal trust. The team is generally capable and basic expectations of the team are usually met, but the team may have become very comfortable with the way it does things and not energised to go above and beyond what is expected in any way. As a result, new team members can find it hard to be accepted and trusted by the team unless they conform to that group's way of working, diversity is not welcomed and in particular, anything that suggests change (e.g. new ideas) is resisted due to the team's lack of energy.

Functioning team — The team is generally working well, has strong capabilities, is likely to be delivering on its objectives and doing what is expected. Team members know their roles, trust each other and their manager and interact well when it is necessary to co-operate on tasks. However, the team is unlikely ever to do anything over and above expectations, or to look beyond what is expected to the broader value it could be delivering for the organisation. As a result, all of the team's energy is internally focused, which may result in it operating in a siloed manner. Team members are unlikely to engage with the broader organisation, leading to limited trust in stakeholders external to the team.

Superior team — The team works in an agile and flexible manner, with team members fully capable of taking on multiple roles within the team and adapting to situations as they arise. This team is energised to over-achieve on most of its objectives and adds value beyond the team to the broader organisation. As a result, the performance of the team far exceeds what individuals could achieve on their own, and the level of trust in team members, their reputations and capabilities are significantly enhanced by being part of the team.

In the context of team performance, quantum leadership is about the excitation of a sudden and significant leap from wherever a team is currently sitting in the hierarchy of needs to a higher state of being.

Organisational quantum levels

Organisations as a whole also exist at quantum levels depending on their degree of evolution and maturity, the environments in which they operate, and their cultures, which are heavily influenced by the leadership being demonstrated at all levels of each organisation. Organisational quantum levels can be summarised as follows:

MEANING

Need: Making a positive difference in the world, service and responsibility, aspiration, innovation and creativity

ACHIEVEMENT

Need: Accomplishing goals, quality systems and processes, pride in performance, customer satisfaction

BELONGING

Need: A sense of corporate community, loyalty, friendship, fun

SECURITY

Need: Feeling of psychological safety, culture of inclusion and accountability

SURVIVAL

Need: Financial stability, goals in place, functions and resources in place and organised

The quantum level at which an organisation exists will be the level below that at which the needs are not being met. Organisational quantum levels can be described as follows:

Survival — An organisation existing in this state is struggling for survival. Its financial state is likely to be highly unstable, and it will be underperforming to an extent that makes it unable to properly build capabilities, resource and organise itself. As a result, the organisation will have a very short-term focus on money and no real focus on its purpose or longer-term goals. The culture is likely to be highly reactive, risk averse, and money centric.

Security — An organisation existing in this state is trying to maintain the status quo and feels threatened by disruptions that are going on around it. Diversity and innovation are probably talked about but are not practised, with a strong preference for sticking with 'the way we've always done things'; anything different will be perceived as a threat and will most likely be rejected by the 'organisational immune system'. As a result, there is likely to be a culture of 'blame' when things go wrong and 'claim' when things go right. These are all driven by a fear of failure (lack of trust) and a need for people to continually justify their existence (waste of energy).

Belonging — An organisation existing in this state is trying to find its place in its market, its community and potentially in its own broader organisation (typical in multi-nationals). At some level, these organisations feel undervalued in their ecosystems (capabilities are not recognised) and are constantly trying to convince that ecosystem of their value and worth (want to be trusted). As a result, people in these organisations may spend a lot of energy constantly talking up their own organisation or teams and criticising other organisations or teams. These organisations can also be overly sensitive to criticism and feedback that is anything other than positive.

Achievement — An organisation existing in this state is delivering solid and sustained results. It is likely to be holding a strong position in its market due to its capabilities and delivering excellent value to its customers and stakeholders (building trust). There is likely to be a strong sense of confidence and energy throughout the organisation which leads to a greater appetite for risk-taking and setting stretch goals. The organisation is also likely to be able to afford to invest in excellent resources and the development of people, as well as developing quality systems and processes to lock in its sustained performance (building and sustaining capability). These organisations need to be careful not to become overconfident and susceptible to disruption. This can happen if they become too focused on their own achievements and fail to keep an eye on the evolving trends in their industries and markets.

Meaning — An organisation existing in this state is likely to have locked in sustained over-performance over the long term in all elements of its 'balanced scorecard'. Outstanding financial performance enables the organisation to invest heavily in its community, its people, its customer service, its processes and procedures, its research and development, and in innovation and creativity more generally. These things in turn feed back into more outstanding financial performance and return for stakeholders, as well as continually building capabilities and trust. As a result, people in such an organisation are highly energised and have a strong sense that they are working towards something that is truly valuable and contributing to shaping a better world.

In the organisational context, quantum leadership is about the excitation of a sudden, significant leap from wherever the organisation currently sits in this hierarchy of needs to a higher state of being.

The quantum equation

A major determinant of the quantum level of any entity is the presence or absence of the core factors of capability, trust and energy. I believe these core factors provide the key to a new leadership concept.

At the heart of quantum leadership theory is an equation, I call it the 'quantum equation', which differentiates this concept of leadership from other more traditional theories. Indeed, it is through this equation that we can answer the question, 'How can I generate a sudden, significant improvement in performance in individuals and/or teams and/or entire organisations in response to the rapidly changing environment in which we are working?'

The quantum equation is:

$$Q = C \times T^2 \times E^2$$

where

Q = the **quantum performance level** of an individual, team, or organisation

C = the level of **capability** applied by an individual, team, or organisation

T = the level of **trust** felt in and by an individual, team, or organisation

E = the level of **energy** felt in and by an individual, team, or organisation

To understand how this equation points to a different and deliberate approach that leaders can take in response to the unpredictable and sometimes chaotic nature of quantum environments, let's look at some of the simple but powerful features of the equation.

First, this equation is very deliberately a multiplication equation.

There are two primary reasons for this.

1. If any of the factors (things we are multiplying together) is zero, the answer is zero! This means that all three elements must have a positive value for there to be any overall value at all. So, in practice, from a leadership perspective, each of these values must be present in an individual, team or organisation for it to be performing at a level higher than the lowest quantum level ($Q = 0$ equates to the lowest quantum level). For example, a team that has high levels of trust among its members and is highly energised to achieve its goals can still be performing at the lowest quantum level if it does not have the required capabilities within the team to achieve its objectives

2. When all three components are in place, the effect is far more than just the sum of the three parts — there is a definite multiplier or magnification effect! It is critical to understand this point because it is central to the practical application of quantum leadership. To excite a quantum leap in performance, if you can somehow increase all three of these components (capability, trust, and energy) at the same time, even by a small amount, there can be a sudden and significant improvement in the performance of the individual, team or organisation.

The other important mathematical feature of the quantum equation is the fact that the trust and energy factors are squared. This is also very deliberate and highlights the importance of the unrealised potential that is locked away within any individual, team or organisation — that is, the capabilities, talents, strengths, ideas, thoughts and creativity which people, for whatever reason, have decided not yet to reveal. Trust and energy are squared to emphasise how much an individual's, team's or organisation's performance can lift when these components are present to a high degree.

From our extensive experience, my colleagues and I at Executive Central know that every organisation already has within its own people the potential to achieve virtually anything it could want. The challenge is how to unlock that potential. When you think about it, the only way individuals will ever unlock their full potential is if they decide to do this themselves. No-one else can force an individual to release their full potential. It is my belief that the amount of their own potential that individuals will unlock, or release, is determined by the amount of trust they feel (in themselves, their relationships and their environments), and how energised they feel (both physically and mentally). When people feel both trust and energy, it is astonishing how much individual potential is translated into actual performance.

It should be noted that allowing any of the factors of the quantum equation to diminish will reduce the level of performance of any entity. It is also possible to produce a negative quantum leap in performance if the three components are diminished simultaneously in the immediate/short term. It might seem unimaginable that anyone would ever allow this to happen, but I have seen it happen many times when leaders have failed to properly think through the impact of their decisions. The results of a negative quantum leap in performance can be devastating and take years to recover from.

To ensure we are exciting positive quantum leaps and avoiding negative ones, it is vital for leaders to understand each of the three factors of the quantum equation — capability, trust and energy — and how they are at play for each entity in every leadership situation they confront. The key to exciting a quantum leap in performance is to find a way to increase all three factors (capability, trust and energy) simultaneously by identifying a purposeful strategy for each entity they are focusing on. The next chapters will explore impactful ways in which leaders can increase the level of capability, trust and energy in any individual, team or organisation in the immediate or short term.

CHAPTER 2

Quantum leadership foundations

Like any well-built house, if you want to set yourself up for success as an executive leader, it is vital that you build your 'leadership house' on very solid foundations. It really does not matter what else you put on top of the house, if the foundation is not solid your leadership will come tumbling down like a house of cards the moment the going gets tough!

I see this scenario a lot in the leadership space, where barely a week goes by without someone coming out with a new theory or concept. These leadership theories are often quite seductive. Anyone involved in leadership, or leadership development, can very easily get swept up in the excitement around these new theories and spend a great deal of time, energy and money trying to force-fit them to their workplace. The reason these (often more advanced) theories are sometimes ineffectual is because leaders do not have their fundamental practices and capabilities properly honed. To extend the house analogy, there is not much point adding a second storey to your house if its foundation is already struggling to hold up the first storey!

So, what are these fundamental practices and capabilities?

I–We–You leadership

To simplify the often complicated subject area of organisational leadership, at Executive Central we have developed a leadership framework that we call the 'I–We–You' leadership model. This model incorporates many of the key themes of most of the highly regarded and well-used contemporary leadership models but attempts to organise them into a capability framework that makes sense to busy organisational leaders.

Simply put, there are three levels of leadership that every leader needs to build capabilities in: I-leadership, We-leadership and You-leadership. You can picture this model as the layers of an onion, with I-leadership in the centre of the onion, We-leadership as the next layer, and You-leadership as the outer layer.

Our I | We | You *leadership framework*

Competencies developed:

- Self awareness
- Self management
- Self development
- Decision making skills
- Problem solving
- Managerial courage
- Professional practice
- Integrity

- Building internal and external relationship
- Client and stakeholder focus
- Teamwork
- Inclusive leadership
- Driving and monitoring performance
- Building individual and organisational capabilities
- Inspiring people at all levels

I
Developing critical self-leadership capabilities

We
Developing and leveraging the capabilities and efforts of others.

You
Unlocking the potential of all stakeholders in the organisational ecosystem

- Strategic thinking
- Strategic leadership
- Networking
- Navigating complexity
- Adaptation
- Implementing change
- Innovation
- Business improvement
- Business acumen
- Corporate risk management

I-leadership

There are some very important capabilities that sit in the I-leadership level, including self-awareness, self-management, self-development, decision-making skills, problem-solving skills, managerial courage, professional practice, and integrity. Leaders must be self-starting, they must manage their own time and priorities, and they must be prepared to lead by example. To do all of these things, good leaders must have high levels of energy, motivation and drive and need to be self-confident and self-motivated people. Without these attributes, leaders cannot effectively lead themselves, let alone anyone else.

If, however, leaders fail to move beyond the I-leadership level (we call these people 'I-leaders') they are really limited to being, at best, high-performing individual contributors. I-leaders tend to be very self-focused and less concerned about other people. I-leaders tend to need to be in control because they believe no-one else can possibly do things as well as them. They love to have their fingers on the pulse of everything that is happening and be the decision makers. They love to be in the spotlight, getting recognised or congratulated for their great work. But when things are not going so well, I-leaders tend to find a way to be out of the limelight. They expect everyone else's priorities to change to suit their own ever-changing priorities. They like to have others running around arranging things for them and seemingly filling every available minute in their day with meetings and tasks, which, of course, makes them look and feel very important.

I-leaders, no matter how good they are in their own particular field, always end up becoming bottlenecks in an organisation because each of them is only one person. They fail to recognise the fundamental concept that leadership is about leveraging the strengths, talents, abilities and energy of *other* people. Do the maths: one person working at 100 per cent effectiveness and efficiency versus six people (a typical team size) working at 50 per cent effectiveness and efficiency is three times less effective and efficient. Just imagine what is possible when the team members start working at more than half their potential!

Indeed, in my experience it is not inaccurate to state that many people in management and leadership roles who display the traits of I-leaders are not actually behaving as leaders at all! They are behaving more as technical or functional experts who happen to have other people reporting to them. We need leaders to move beyond I-leadership, which brings us to the next layer of the onion.

We-leadership

When they reach the We-leadership level, organisational leaders make an extremely important next step: they begin to leverage other people! Indeed, the central positive attribute of We-leadership is an ability to create a sense of shared purpose among a group of people and rally those people around that cause. In short, people possessing We-leadership capabilities are good at building a team of people around them who are very loyal, very committed and typically, very energised about what the team and its leader are trying to accomplish.

We-leadership requires a leader to have higher levels of emotional intelligence. At this level, leaders move beyond self-awareness and become aware of others and how they like to operate. They can then adapt their approach and create a setting to suit the preferences of other people, which enables them to get better results with these people who also feel more comfortable when they are working together. They also tend to be good at leading teams, setting shared priorities for the team, harnessing the diversity of the team's members, and running efficient and effective team processes. As such, they have well-developed competencies in building relationships, client and stakeholder focus, teamwork, driving and monitoring performance, building both individual and organisational capabilities, and inspiring people at both an individual and collective level. People working for leaders who possess these capabilities tend to find being a member of that team a very exciting and rewarding experience.

However, problems start surfacing when leaders get stuck at the We-leadership level and fail to move beyond it (we call these people 'we-leaders'). While being on the inside of a we-leader's team can be great, try being on the outside of it. We-leaders tend to create a feeling of 'us and them' where people within the team are encouraged to view people outside of the team with some suspicion. Often, we-leaders like their team to compete with other teams in the organisation to be the 'best' and, in extreme cases, will even create a kind of 'siege mentality' within their own teams which makes that team try harder to win. This need to win can manifest as the team being incredibly hard to deal with inside the organisation. If an organisation has issues with what is commonly called 'silo mentality', there is a good chance that one or more we-leaders are involved.

All of these problems come from the fact that there still tends to be a lot of 'I' in a we-leader's psychology. Instead of 'me and my achievements' of an I-leader, the language changes to 'my team and our achievements', but the we-leader still has a strong need for recognition and approval (typically from superiors) and is still highly internally competitive.

I can speak with a great deal of authority about We-leadership because for a very large part of my corporate career, I was the world's biggest we-leader. Early in my career at Compaq Computer Australia, I was asked, with my colleague Geoff Anson, to form the Consumer Division in Australia. This division was set up in the early 1990s to sell computers to the home market through retailers, something Compaq had never done before. We were the new kids on the block and in the early days, we took our fair share of friendly jibes from the more established divisions within the company about the size and style of our business. They really were just friendly jibes, but I took them as personal ridicule and was determined to show the 'big boys' by knocking them off their perches and becoming the top division in the entire company.

So, for the next seven or so years, I did all the things we-leaders tend to do. I built a terrific team of people, rallied them around the cause of building the Consumer Division into the top division, and created an atmosphere of loyalty, enthusiasm and energy. This also coincided with explosive growth in our business as the home computer market took off throughout the 1990s. I also created a 'siege mentality' with respect to the rest of the organisation and this rubbed off on many of my team. We really saw other divisions as the enemy trying to get in our way at every opportunity. Indeed, the rest of the organisation knew us as 'Fortress Consumer' because we were such a difficult group to deal with — something I didn't know until years later! All of this was further evidence of the 'siege mentality' we had created.

Ultimately, this kind of internally competitive, unproductive behaviour ends up limiting the effectiveness of a we-leader. A we-leader may be better at leveraging the abilities and energy of other people — their own team — but they fail to unlock the full potential of the entire organisation. This then brings us to the final layer of the onion.

You-leadership

You-leaders possess all of the positive attributes I have described for I-leadership and We-leadership but they make the final, and most important, step of them all. They realise that leadership is not about the leader, it is about those who are being led. You-leaders recognise that the fundamental role of a leader is to try to unlock the full potential of those who they lead and that this will only ever happen if those people choose to let their own potential out. In other words, it is the people being led (the 'you' in You-leadership) who will ultimately decide whether to give their best effort, share their creativity, solve problems, delight customers, apply their expertise, etc. It is the leader's role to create an environment that helps them make that decision.

The key difference that distinguishes a you-leader from a we-leader is that they have far greater levels of self-esteem, self-confidence and self-actualisation. Put simply, they are 'comfortable in their own skin' and do not rely on the approval of others to determine whether they are successful or not. A you-leader determines success from evidence and facts, and their own sense of achievement. Rather than seeking the approval of others, they prefer to earn the respect of others.

You-leaders also display high levels of humility. This means they are not afraid to admit when they do not know something or when they have made a mistake. Indeed, a you-leader embraces both of these situations as opportunities to learn and explore options and to unlock the creativity and problem-solving abilities of both themselves and others around them. Furthermore, you-leaders are happy to let others take the lead when this will result in the best outcome.

You-leaders are able to apply themselves to higher order aspects of leadership such as strategic thinking, strategic leadership, networking, navigating complexity, adaptation, implementing change, innovation, improvement, business acumen and corporate risk management.

It may seem that what I am suggesting as the attributes of you-leaders are all too good to be true and that such a person sounds 'perfect' and could not possibly exist. However, it is the very fact that you-leaders know that they are not 'perfect' themselves that makes them capable of achieving you-leader status. You-leaders know that it is a combination of the different strengths of team members that represents the almost unlimited potential any organisation has at its disposal. It is the you-leader who continually strives to find new ways of combining these strengths and creating an environment that unlocks this potential.

I like to think of the I-We-You leadership model as defining a journey to leadership for any leader. Looking at all of the capabilities and how they fit into the model, it is clear that we could fill many books in discussing how to develop every one of these. I believe, though, there are some core leadership capabilities that enable many of the other capabilities called for at all levels of the model. These core, or 'foundational', capabilities are most definitely critical to quantum leaders.

So, what are these foundational capabilities? The answer is provided by this simple and pragmatic definition of leadership that my colleagues and I use when working with leaders at all levels: 'When you boil it all down, leadership is really about *achieving things with and through other people!'*

I believe there are three foundational capabilities: priority management, motivational and developmental delegation, and emotional intelligence. For the remainder of this chapter, I will focus on each of these capabilities in detail.

Priority management

All leadership is about 'achieving things'. The question is, what things? Obviously, at the most senior levels of leadership in organisations, leaders need to decide on a vision or purpose for the organisation and develop strategies that will then deliver it. Clearly, the ability to develop strategies that take into account the complex environments within which organisations operate is a critical skill for senior leaders. More fundamentally, however, when a strategy has been determined, the ability to execute that strategy requires leaders at all levels to be able to prioritise (and de-prioritise) effectively, to make most effective use of the resources they have available to them.

The five levers of business acumen

The resources that leaders have available to them are finite. No matter how much we try, we cannot get around the fact that there is only so much time available, only so many people available, and only so many capital resources available. Indeed, for a leader to have the most basic level of business acumen, he or she needs to realise that there are only five possible decisions that can be made when it comes to running a business. I like to call these the five 'levers' of business acumen.

Fundamental rule of management

There are only five possible levers you can pull and they are all linked

SCOPE RESOURCES TIME BUDGET QUALITY

You simply cannot vary the settings of any one of these without at least one of the others needing to change also...

Scope lever

Leaders need to decide how much their organisations are going to try to do i.e. which activities or projects will be undertaken. Leaders can push the lever forward to increase the scope of work being attempted, or they can pull it back to reduce the scope of work being attempted.

Resources lever

Leaders need to decide how many people and/or how many other resources (e.g. equipment) they are going to allocate to each element of the scope of works that has been decided on. Leaders can push the lever forward to increase the resources allocated to a task (which may require recruitment of new people or purchasing new resources, or re-allocation of existing resources from other tasks), or pull it back to reduce the resources allocated.

Time lever

Leaders need to decide how much time they are going to allow for the achievement of the scope of works that has been decided on. Leaders can push the lever forward to increase the amount of time being allowed or pull it back to reduce the amount of time being allowed.

Budget lever

Leaders need to decide how much money they are going to commit to the scope of works that has been decided on. Leaders can push the lever forward to increase the budget or pull it back to reduce the budget.

Quality lever

Leaders need to decide what level of quality is required for the scope of works that has been decided on. Leaders can push the lever forward to increase the quality (e.g. output needs to be of Rolls Royce quality with every possible element perfect) or pull the lever back to reduce the quality (e.g. we only need a minimum viable product or a draft quality output).

Using the levers

While each of these five decisions that leaders need to consider are separate and discrete, they are all interconnected and impact on each other. I like to think of the five separate levers as having a rubber band connecting them. Whenever one lever is moved, the rubber band will try to move at least one other lever to keep the tension in equilibrium.

The "rubber band" metaphor
All five levers are connected by a tensioned rubber band

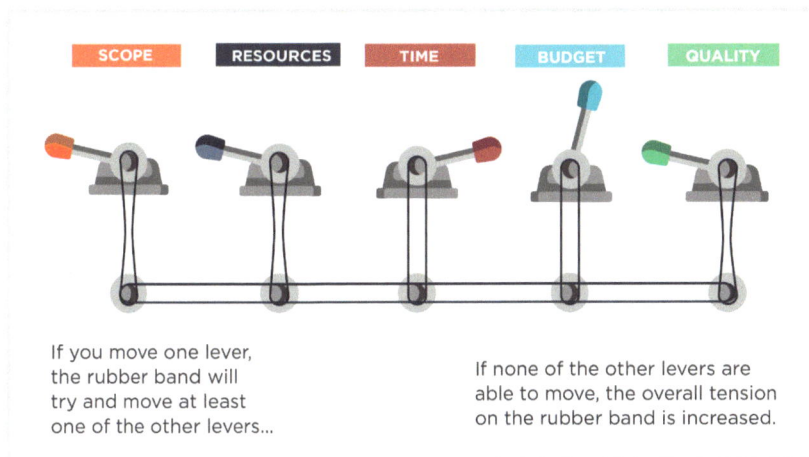

SCOPE · RESOURCES · TIME · BUDGET · QUALITY

If you move one lever, the rubber band will try and move at least one of the other levers...

If none of the other levers are able to move, the overall tension on the rubber band is increased.

It will either successfully move at least one of the other levers (often more than one) or, if no other lever is moved, the overall tension of the rubber band is increased.

It is, of course, possible to increase the tension on a rubber band by stretching it further. Indeed, there needs to be tension of some kind on the rubber band for it to be of any use. Without tension, it is just a useless piece of rubber. Stretching it further actually increases the energy stored in it and increases the force it can produce. However, if it is stretched beyond its elastic limit, it will snap and thereby revert to a useless piece of rubber. So, it is fair to say that perhaps a sixth decision that leaders need to make is the level of tension they want to apply to their organisations. They can increase the tension in the system, or they can decrease it.

As a simple example, if a leader decides to add a new project to their team's scope of works, there will likely be a need for some more time to achieve this project on top of the projects the team is already trying to deliver. If more time is not available, then perhaps more resources will be required, which in turn might require more money in the budget. If no more time, resources or budget are available, then perhaps a decision could be made to reduce the overall quality of work being delivered in order to get everything done. If none of these are options, then the overall tension in the organisation will be increased to try to allow for the new project without any change to any other lever.

The point is, it is impossible to change the setting of any one lever without there being a corresponding change in the overall settings of other levers and/or the tension of the overall system. Unfortunately, what I have seen happen over and over again in organisations is the situation where leaders will make a decision to change the setting of one lever without then taking any time to consider what other decisions need to be made. In my experience, there are two common outcomes of this behaviour.

The first outcome is that the other levers change anyway whether the leader likes it or not. This means things like deadlines get missed, budgets blow out, or quality diminishes. The second outcome is that the tension or stress levels in the organisation are significantly increased over a sustained period of time. This increased level of stress then increases the risk in the business (e.g. mistakes get made, things get missed), reduces the wellbeing and resilience of people, and reduces the sustainability of all resources. Basically, either of these outcomes can have dramatic impacts on a business and all point to very poor leadership and management practices.

Prioritisation as a foundation

In defence of leaders, in the 24/7 world of IT and telecommunications, the sheer volume of things that can compete for the attention of a leader is immense. (Right now, you might even be wondering what has dropped into your email inbox in the last few minutes!) The ability to prioritise for themselves, their teams and their organisations is therefore a foundational skill for leaders. Over the many years that I have been an executive coach, the issue of priority management has been one of the most common challenges faced by the leaders with whom I have worked. I will go so far as to say that I think it is a universal challenge for all leaders. Because of its foundational nature, the skill of prioritisation is required, for different reasons, across the entire I-We-You leadership paradigm.

At the I-leadership level, leaders must be able to prioritise (and de-prioritise) what they spend their own time doing. In about 2005, I was fortunate enough to hear the then CEO of AMP Ltd, Craig Dunne, address a group of emerging executives for whom I was conducting a leadership development program. He said to them, 'The most valuable gift you have to give as a leader is your time'. He then went on to say that where leaders spend their time says far more about what they truly consider important than anything they say. I cannot agree more with Craig! The problem is, there are so many things competing for leaders' time and attention that if they do not prioritise effectively, they are not leading anything. Instead, they are just rushing around, reacting to other people's agendas.

At the We-leadership level, leaders must be able to prioritise (and de-prioritise) what their teams spend their time doing. They must also ensure that individual team members are prioritising their own time effectively to ensure the overall team priorities are being achieved. This includes helping team members prioritise and delegate tasks and responsibilities effectively to their teams, and so on. I will revisit the topic of delegation shortly. But leaders cannot delegate effectively if they have not first prioritised effectively.

At the You-leadership level, prioritisation takes on a far greater level of complexity. Deciding on organisational priorities requires a far greater depth of thinking about what is truly important to the organisation, what will have the greatest impact for customers and other stakeholders, what will reduce risk most effectively, what will best utilise available assets, and what will ready the organisation for the inevitable changes that will occur in its operating environment. It also requires a level of business acumen to help filter out distractions that may seem mission critical when someone is jumping up and down about them or creating a fuss, but which really do not add a lot of value to the organisation in the long run.

Priority management methods

There are hundreds of books that have been written about time and priority management, so I do not intend to cover the topic in huge detail. What I will share, though, are some of the quick wins that I believe can make a huge difference for leaders at all levels of the I-We-You leadership spectrum.

Prioritisation vs to-do lists

The first major change leaders need to make is to move away from what are effectively 'to-do lists' and create priority lists. To-do lists can take many forms, but for the purposes of this discussion they are essentially any un-prioritised list of tasks or projects which in any way attract the attention of a leader and require action from that leader.

A terrific example of a modern to-do list is the email inbox. This is just a list of emails that are received in an un-prioritised manner and which will definitely attract the attention of and require action from most leaders.

A prioritised list requires the leader to consider each task or project and deliberately prioritise it. By definition, to prioritise something is to give it precedence in order, by rank, etc. To be able to do this, a leader needs some basis for deciding the order or rank of tasks or projects. We will come to this process in a moment.

Before considering prioritisation methods, it is important to realise that regardless of the method used to prioritise things, every time something is made a priority, by definition something else is deprioritised (i.e. pushed back in the order or rank of things). In my experience, many leaders have discussions within their organisations about priorities but they do not have discussions specifically about what will be deprioritised as a result of this prioritisation. People within the organisation are often left to their own devices to determine what must be deprioritised in order to make way for the new priority. The problem with this is that people will often just assume everything is a top priority, and we are back to the point of having a whole lot of un-prioritised to-do lists. In short, if everything is a priority, then nothing is a priority!

As I have already discussed, in a quantum environment things can change for leaders very quickly. As such, priorities also need to change to react to these environmental changes. I believe that a mission critical skill for quantum leaders is not only their ability to prioritise things effectively, but also their ability to decide and clearly articulate what things are deprioritised to correspond with each new priority. When this is done effectively, so much time, effort and money can be saved in avoiding the confusion that can reign when priorities are unclear.

How to prioritise

There are many methods that can be used to assist in the prioritisation of tasks and projects but in my experience, the simplest and most effective is the 'urgency vs importance' matrix. I first came across this many years ago when I read *Seven habits of highly effective people* by Stephen R. Covey, and then again in a time and priority management course I attended when I was first promoted to a management role. I am sure many leaders will have come across this model from time to time, but I wonder how many leaders actively use it regularly. My guess would be very few based on what I see day-to-day in many organisations.

The concept is simple. Leaders need to rate a task or project based on its degree of importance (either highly important or less important) and its degree of urgency (either highly urgent or less urgent). While these two terms seem simple enough, to ensure they are used according to the intent of this prioritisation method, they both warrant some further discussion.

When we consider the 'importance' dimension, there are many things that could define something as being important. In this case, the intention is to rate something in terms of its impact on what the leader is expected to deliver. In other words, how significant is this activity to the delivery of the leader's own key performance indicators (KPIs)? Obviously, depending on what lens is being used for the prioritisation, these KPIs could be individual, team or organisational KPIs. For something to be rated as highly important, it must have a high impact on at least one of these KPIs. It is probably fair to say that someone who is a you-leader would rank impact on organisational KPIs higher than impact on team KPIs, and impact on team KPIs as higher than impact on individual KPIs. It is easy to see that the deeper one dives into any prioritisation methodology, the more complex it can become.

When we then consider the 'urgency' dimension, most people understand that for something to be considered urgent, there is usually some kind of time pressure or deadline associated with it. I find it more interesting to consider the source of the time pressure or deadline. In my experience, most things that are regarded as urgent usually have someone else involved in creating the time pressure. This could be someone's boss, a client, a key stakeholder, or even some kind of regulator or authority. One thing I like to challenge my coachees to do is to consider whether the time pressure is actually being created by that other person, or whether it is being imagined or assumed based on the other person's position or seniority.

Consider this example. I recently held a leadership workshop for a government department where we were discussing the topic of prioritisation and the concepts of importance and urgency. During that discussion, one of the participants made the statement that sometimes things can be urgent even though they do not have a pressing deadline associated with them. When I asked him to elaborate, he gave the example that any task that comes from their minister's office is immediately considered urgent. Many of the people in the audience began nodding their heads in agreement. When I questioned further, he indicated that any other project or task would be deprioritised to make way for the task from the minister's office, just to keep the minister happy! When I asked whether this kind of practice had any kind of detrimental impact on the quality of work being delivered on key projects by the department, he indicated that it absolutely did, but that was just the way things rolled in the department. Again, there were a lot of heads nodding in agreement.

Here is a fascinating example of 'assumed urgency'. The staff of this department were assuming that anything that came from the minister's office (which, by the way, most of the time is not actually the minister himself/herself) was automatically urgent. From a prioritisation perspective, this behaviour actually had the effect of deprioritising key projects, which had already been signed off as ministerial priorities, in order to make a priority out of anything else they saw coming from the minister. In this case, some of the tasks that were coming from the minister's office may well have been highly important because they had a high impact on what the department was meant to deliver (although I suspect many of them were not very important either!) but that does not mean they also had to be urgent.

My very strong advice to leaders when using this prioritisation method is to ensure that anything that is being rated as highly urgent does in fact have a true deadline, not an imagined or assumed one!

Once activities have been rated on the 'importance and urgency' scales, they can be plotted on the quadrant model shown opposite.

The process of transferring the prioritised tasks or projects into this model is simple. It is actually the next phase that is far more important. This phase considers what priority the leader is going to give to each quadrant. Over the years, I have spoken to many audiences about this model. I ask the question, 'Which quadrant do you think you would do first?' Almost everyone immediately answers that they would do the top right quadrant first. I then ask the question, 'Which quadrant do you think you would do last?' Almost everyone immediately answers that they would do the bottom left quadrant last. I completely agree with these answers and so does just about anyone — including Stephen R. Covey — who has ever considered them.

The next question I ask is, 'Which quadrant do you think you should

Achieving things

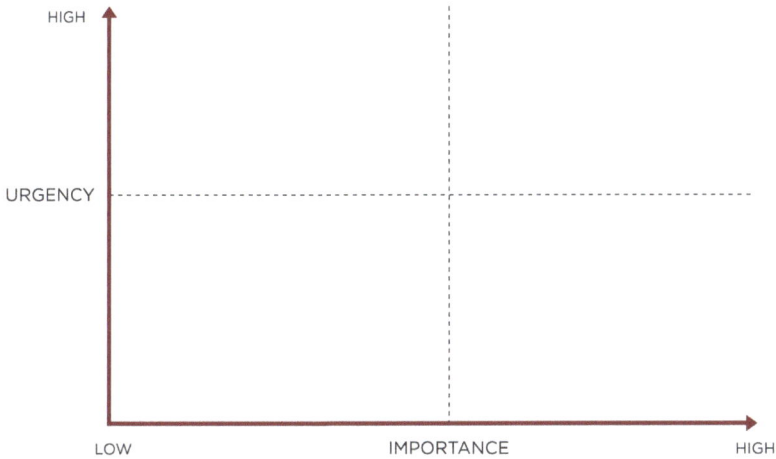

do second?' At this point, there is usually quite a lengthy pause and sometimes an audible 'Mmm …' while the audience considers the model. Then, I usually get about a fifty-fifty split in the responses. Half of the audience will say that the bottom right quadrant should be done second and the other half will say that the top left should be done second. Before discussing this any further, I then ask my final question which is, 'Which quadrant do you actually do second?' The response rate changes to about a ninety-ten split. About 90 per cent of people admit that they would do the top left quadrant second and the bottom right third. In other words, 90 per cent of people prioritise highly urgent but unimportant tasks above highly important but not urgent tasks. This is where we discover a major problem in the way most people work!

As anyone who has read any of Stephen R. Covey's teachings will know, in prioritisation theory the correct answer to the question of which quadrant should come second is the bottom right, highly important but not urgent tasks. See the illustration over the page. From a leadership perspective, I think it is fair to say that virtually every good leadership practice or behaviour that has ever been written about or taught was not really meant to be done urgently. As such, these leadership best practices really should sit in the bottom right quadrant. The problem is, if people are giving priority to the top left quadrant, this often is not where these practices sit. Let's consider this a little more deeply.

Achieving things

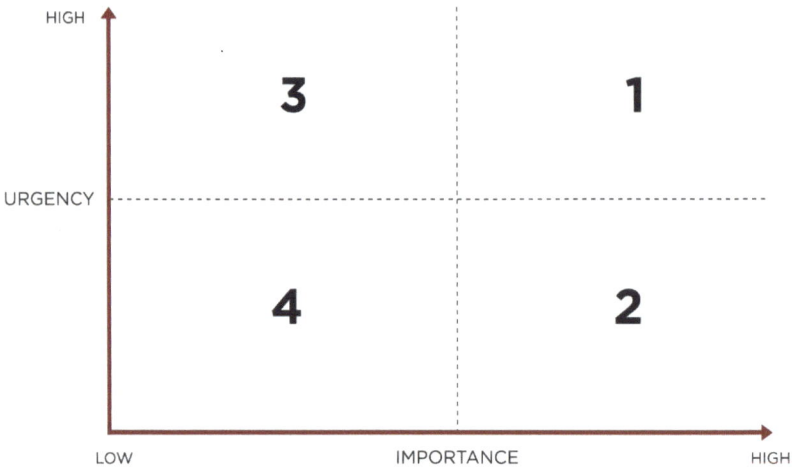

If I describe my experience of the type of work that finds its way into the highly urgent but unimportant category (quadrant 3), the word that I think sums it up is 'busy'. This type of work has people rushing around, scrambling to get things done quickly, almost in a kind of panic. It also sees people with diaries full of meetings, being called in for urgent discussions and generally looking like they are working very hard. People who habitually work this way tend to be quite stressed and, if they are leaders, tend to create a lot of stress for people with whom they work. Obviously, this way of operating in and of itself can cause many problems within organisations.

The biggest problem with this way of working is that while people are rushing around being busy in quadrant 3, the activities that sit in the bottom right quadrant (quadrant 2) which are highly important but not urgent, tend to get put off. Many of these tasks are likely to require a good deal of thought and might take a significant amount of time to complete. However, it is very hard to commit this time and effort while rushing around in a panic, and so these tasks get delayed. The problem is, they keep getting put off, and put off again, because more and more highly urgent but not important tasks are given priority.

I think back to the first time and priority management course I did in the early 1990s and remember fondly how the trainer made us all laugh when she talked to us about the disease of 'rollitis'. She said that you know you have got a case of rollitis when you find that important tasks on your to-do list tend to roll over from one day to the next, and then one week to the next and so on. This is exactly what people who give priority to quadrant 3 over quadrant 2 tend to suffer from — rollitis!

The problem with continually avoiding or delaying quadrant 2 activities is that they do not go away. What happens if they are put off long enough is that they simply 'float' up into quadrant 1 and become highly urgent as well as highly important. In this scenario, everything that is being worked on, regardless of whether it is important or not, is being done urgently. This is a little bit like running an engine on its red line constantly. The engine will take it only for so long and then, eventually, something will break!

The most common trap

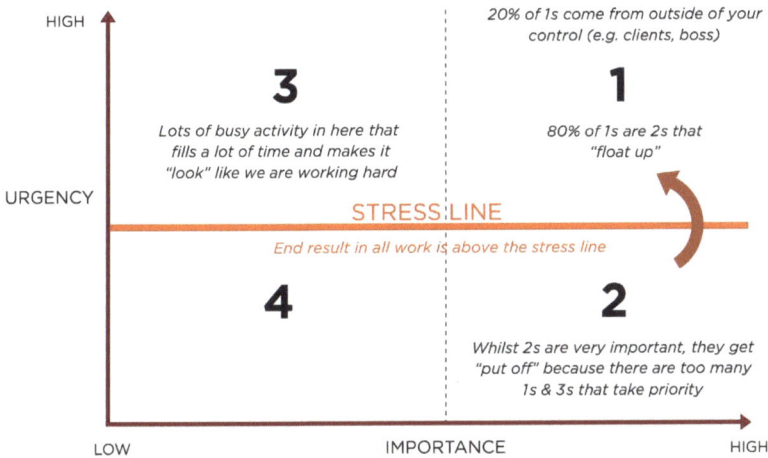

If we consider quadrant 1, it is fair to say that some activities do start off life as both highly important and highly urgent and, in my experience, these might come from an individual's superiors, customers or other key stakeholders. But in reality, of all the activities that are in quadrant 1, I am prepared to accept that at most 20 per cent of them actually started off as quadrant 1. The other 80 per cent of quadrant 1 activities actually started off as quadrant 2 activities, but they were put off for so long that they eventually became urgent and 'floated' into quadrant 1.

If consideration is given to the key leadership practices referred to earlier, there is a significant difference between getting them done in quadrant 2 or letting them become urgent and doing them in quadrant 1. If any leadership practice is not applied until it becomes urgent, the quality and effectiveness of that practice will most likely be much poorer. Let's just consider strategy as an easy example. I have seen plenty of strategies that have been pulled together urgently, but none of them have been what could be considered top-quality strategies. The urgency with which they are created means that there is no time to fully appraise the situation at hand and the needs of the organisation and its stakeholders. There is no time to consider multiple options, develop fall back plans, conduct detailed research, analysis and due diligence on proposed strategies, and so on. All of these quality factors require time to complete and when things are urgent, there is no time. The same applies to any other leadership practice you can name.

Executing priorities

Once the process of sorting all tasks and projects into their correct quadrant has been completed, the next step is to convert these priorities into an execution plan.

In the context of quantum leadership, it is fair to say that the principal objective of priority management is to ensure individuals, teams and organisations are getting important activities done before they become urgent, and leaders are getting their own leadership practices executed before they become urgent. Again, there are myriad priority management strategies that have been proposed in many books and courses, so I will just focus on a few that I believe can have an immediate positive effect for quantum leaders.

Sizing quadrant 1 and 2 activities

One common characteristic of activities that are highly important is that they are likely to require some quality time to get them completed in a quality fashion. As such, once a task has been identified as being in either quadrant 1 or quadrant 2 of the 'urgency vs importance' model, the first thing a leader should do is attempt to 'size' the task or project by considering the five levers I discussed earlier (scope, time, resource, budget and quality).

In formal project management, this 'sizing' process involves creating a project plan that identifies all of the tasks involved in the project and allocating time, resources and a budget to each of these. This is usually represented in some form of Gantt chart so that the project manager can keep a close eye on the progress of each task and ensure the overall project schedule is kept on track. Project managers will also usually implement a system to ensure each task is being completed to an acceptable quality level and any problems encountered along the way are dealt with promptly.

In practice though, not every 'project', which I define as a group of interrelated tasks leading to a certain outcome, warrants the creation of a formal project plan. As such, let's consider a simple way for leaders to 'size' these types of activities.

My recommendation is that leaders should estimate the time an activity will take — and then double it. This is then the amount of time that will need to be factored into the leader's own schedule, or the team or organisational schedule if that is the lens being used, to successfully complete the task or project. I am proposing a doubling of the estimated time for important tasks because, in my experience, such tasks or projects often involve more than might be apparent up front. The planning fallacy, which is a phenomenon where people tend to underestimate the time it will take to complete future tasks, despite knowledge that previous tasks have generally taken longer than planned, is also alive and well in many organisations I have worked with. It is far better to allow a buffer to ensure all of the unseen elements can be handled and/or any unseen interruptions to the process are allowed for.

Consider quadrant 1 and 2 activities as formal appointments

Once quadrant 1 and 2 activities have been 'sized', they should be transferred into the leader's own diary, or the diaries of the people involved in executing them, as formal, fixed-time appointments. Larger, lengthier activities may need to be transferred into a number of diary blocks of time, but they most definitely still need to become diary entries.

The workdays of most modern organisational leaders revolve completely around their diaries. It is fair to say that the diaries of the majority of organisational leaders with whom I have worked become crammed full of meetings, leaving very little time during the working day to do much else. I will have more to say on this issue shortly, but given this reality, my view is that the only way to make space for important activities is to schedule them into the diary as if they were fixed-time appointments.

In an era when leaders' diaries are often visible to other people, particularly their assistants, putting these highly important activities into the diary as fixed-time appointments sends a message that the time is not available to book for other meetings. It is also important to make sure these appointments are specifically named, not just put in as 'self-time' or 'project time'. My advice would be to label the activity as accurately as possible so that its importance is clear to everyone.

For example, if I had a task that was associated with the preparation for an important client meeting, I would label it as 'preparation for xyz meeting'. This way, if my assistant or anyone else was trying to find a time to slot in another meeting, they would not just book over the top of this time without at least asking. The fact that the meeting is identified expresses some of its importance.

Segment days to allow for all quadrants

While it is critical to allow appropriate time for quadrant 1 and 2 activities, let's not forget that quadrant 2 activities are not urgent and can in fact be scheduled a little further out in leaders' diaries. In other words, leaders do not need to complete every quadrant 1 and 2 activity in the immediate term.

Quadrant 1 activities must be scheduled in the near term due to their urgency. It is therefore important to get them into the diary as soon as possible (i.e. within coming days). But as long as they are sized and scheduled appropriately, and that schedule is adhered to, most quadrant 2 activities can be spread out over weeks and even months. This means that it is not necessary, or wise, to fill an entire day with quadrant 1 and 2 activities.

Because important activities are likely to require some quality thinking and application from leaders, it is actually far better to limit the time given to them in any one day. Choosing a time when leaders are more likely to be at their best and will have the energy required to commit to these important tasks will give much better results and increase the probability of leaders actually sticking to the plan. Each leader needs to decide for themselves when this is most likely to be, but it is worth noting that I have not seen too many leaders functioning at their best when they have already been in multiple meetings, or have already had to deal with a lot of things on any given day. Further, if time is scheduled for important activities later in the day, there is an increased probability of issues popping up earlier in the day that will distract from or require rescheduling of these activities.

My approach is to schedule from 10 am on most days a period of 2 to 2.5 hours to dedicate to important (quadrant 1 or 2) activities; obviously, there are exceptions from time to time. I know that for me, this time of day is when I do my best thinking work. Each day in my calendar has this slot available and this is where I schedule appointments for specific important activities into my diary. This then allows plenty of space for other fixed-time appointments and other quadrant 3 and 4 activities on any given day.

By sticking to this approach, I have found that it is possible to very quickly deal with quadrant 1 activities and get them completely off my plate. By then dealing with quadrant 2 activities in a disciplined and planned way, before they become urgent, I am able to stop the 'floating' effect of important tasks becoming urgent and moving from quadrant 2 up into quadrant 1. This then has the effect of dramatically reducing the overall number of quadrant 1 activities because, as I discussed earlier, it eliminates the source of 80 per cent of them. This, in turn, results in a significant reduction in the level of stress and urgency in the system, which has many positive flow-on effects.

Filling the rest of the day

If leaders deal with important tasks in the manner that I have suggested, there is plenty of time left on any given day for other meetings and quadrant 3 and 4 activities. It is important that these activities are handled efficiently and effectively so as not to allow them to distract from more important activities or to introduce unwanted levels of stress and urgency into a leader's environment.

On the subject of other meetings — that is, meetings that are not specifically associated with quadrant 1 and 2 activities scheduled somewhere in the two-hour block — I am going to make a suggestion that many of my coachees over the years have thought sounded completely impossible, but which, with some discipline, they have actually found is ultimately very achievable. My suggestion is that if a leader is in any more than three hours of other meetings on a given day, that leader is in 'meeting overload'!

The first step in addressing the 'meeting overload' situation is for leaders to become consciously aware of just how many meetings they are in. Certainly, most leaders I have come across are in many more than three hours of other meetings. It is not uncommon for my coachees to show me diaries where quite literally every available minute of the day is taken up in meetings. My question to anyone for whom this sounds familiar is, 'When do you ever get anything else done?' Sadly, the answer is most often, 'After hours!' I am sure I do not need to say just how much of a recipe for disaster this approach is on so many levels for both work and personal life.

Let's just be clear. Three hours of other meetings on any one day is still an awful lot of meeting time. If the 2 to 2.5 hours that I have previously suggested for important activities (quadrant 1 and 2) are then factored in, as well as say another hour for lunch and other breaks, that makes at least six hours that have been taken up already. Other quadrant 3 and 4 activities, which still need to be done, have not even been factored in yet.

Quadrant 3 and 4 activities can come in many forms. They can be emails, telephone messages, travel-related activities, administrative tasks and many more. My suggestion when dealing with any of these activities is to 'batch process' them. Just like a manufacturing facility that is set up to produce batches of the same item for a period of time, people tend to work more effectively and efficiently when they can focus on the one type of thing for a fixed period of time.

Let me give you an example by focusing on a topic that is a challenge for many people in modern organisational life — dealing with emails! A terrible habit that I see in virtually every office environment is people making email the centre of their attention for the entire day. With the inbox permanently open, often with various notification alarms going off, their attention is continually distracted from anything else they are doing to 'just check' the new email they have received. This equally applies to smart phones, smart watches and smart pads, with people often paying more attention to these devices and texts or tweets or snapchats they just received than they are to the actual people they are meeting with or talking to!

To avoid the stress of email overload and to minimise distraction from other more important activities, my suggestion is that two

30-minute blocks of email 'batch processing' time per day is all that is needed. In 30 minutes of focused email time, it is amazing how many emails can be sorted through, actioned, or separately scheduled as important activities. If two of these 30-minute blocks are allowed in a day, say one in the morning and one in the afternoon, I can almost guarantee that is more than enough to be able to stay on top of the email load.

This same 'batch processing' approach works really well for other quadrant 3 and 4 activities like telephone messages, administration tasks, report writing, etc. If the focus for a period of time stays on one type of task, leaders can be far more efficient and effective in churning through these tasks and therefore not allowing them to get in the way of other more important things.

Motivational and developmental delegation

Another foundational skill that all quantum leaders must have is the ability to delegate effectively. In the context of time and priority management, one critical consideration leaders need to be able to make when sorting through the list of activities that need to be completed is to determine which activities they must do themselves, and which could be completed by other people. The ability to delegate effectively is also one of the key determinants of whether a leader is able to make the transition from I-leadership to We-leadership. When I ask leaders, 'Why don't you delegate more?' I am given many reasons why they simply have to take on key activities themselves. The reasons include any or all of the following: 'It is quicker to just do it myself'; 'Nobody can do it as well as I can'; 'I don't trust people to give it the necessary priority'; 'I don't have time to delegate'; 'My people are already working flat out'; 'I'll lose control of the activity if I delegate it'.

The fact is, some of these answers may well be true, but it is my follow-up question that is really more important. That question is, 'What are you deprioritising to take on this task yourself?' In the case of a leader, I am prepared to bet good money that the activities that are being deprioritised and put off by a leader failing to delegate effectively are actually highly important (but not urgent) leadership activities. I have already described that the consequences of this, from a prioritisation perspective, are that these important leadership activities eventually become urgent and, most likely, are completed with a compromised level of quality. What leaders need to realise is that a failure to delegate to others is actually just another form of failing to prioritise the right activities. All of this significantly reduces a leader's ability to excite any kind of positive quantum leap in performance.

The reasons for not delegating demonstrate some of the assumptions that many leaders make when they think of delegation. First, there is an assumption that once something has been delegated it has gone, and the leader has no more control over it. As I will discuss shortly, that definitely should not always be the case. Of course, if this is their assumption, leaders are hardly likely to delegate anything other than the most basic tasks because the more important tasks cannot be exposed to the risk of failure.

Secondly, these leaders are purely thinking of delegation as a task completion exercise – a way to get things done. I strongly suggest that delegation should also be considered an excellent way both to develop and motivate people. While it might take longer to delegate a task to someone else, and there may be some associated risks in doing this, that person is learning, they are being trusted, and they are being motivated, which builds their energy. Motivational and developmental delegation is actually a contributor to all three factors of the quantum equation and can go a long way to creating the conditions for a quantum leap in performance. It is therefore a crucial capability for quantum leaders.

Three delegation options

I would like to share with you a simple delegation methodology which has helped many of my coachees to expand their delegation skills and have far more activities completed by other people than previously. To explain this methodology, I will use the analogy of a sailing race.

Anyone who has ever sailed or who knows anything about sailing knows that when a sailing vessel sails into the wind, it has to tack. Tacking is a manoeuvre by which the sailing vessel turns its bow toward the wind so that the direction from which the wind blows changes from one side to the other, allowing progress in the desired direction. In effect, this creates a zigzag path as the vessel sails into the wind.

Now, if I was the owner of a sailing vessel and I wanted to let another skipper, whose name is Jane, sail my vessel over a course into the wind, there would be a number of things I would be taking into consideration before determining how I would like Jane to sail that course. I would be thinking of Jane's sailing experience, how expensive my vessel is, how difficult my vessel is to sail, how challenging the course is, and what the weather conditions are on the day. My assessment of any one or a combination of these factors would determine how I would like Jane to sail that course. See the illustration below.

Which way to the finish line?

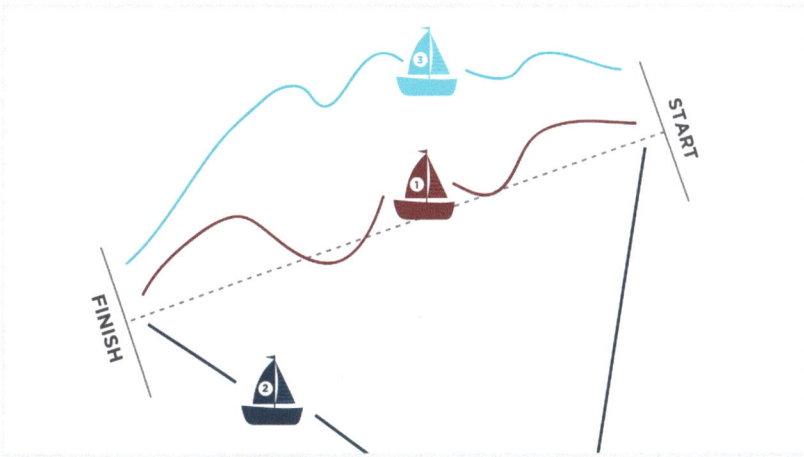

Scenario 1: If Jane is an inexperienced sailor, and/or my vessel is expensive, and/or my vessel is extremely complicated to sail, and/or the course is notoriously tricky with rocks or sand banks to avoid, and/or the weather is particularly threatening, I would probably want Jane to keep the vessel very close to what is known as the layline (the most direct path between the start and finish line). In other words, I really would not want Jane sailing too far off-course at any stage. This means she would need to be regularly tacking to keep the boat close to the layline. The consequence of lots of tacks (or turns) is also to keep the speed of the vessel slower because each tack has a braking effect.

Scenario 2: If Jane is a very experienced sailor, and/or my vessel is inexpensive, and/or it is extremely easy to sail, and/or the course is over a shallow lake with very few dangers, and/or the weather is very calm and stable, I would probably be quite happy to let Jane sail my vessel however she wanted. I would be quite happy for her to sail well away from the layline if she wanted to chase some breeze or build up speed by not tacking the vessel as much.

Scenario 3: In considering any or all of these factors, if I felt the situation was somewhere in between these first two extremes, then perhaps I would want Jane to have some freedom in how she sailed the vessel, but I would still radio in every so often to provide my own advice and check that the vessel was not getting too far off course.

In the context of delegation, the vessel in this analogy is the activity that a leader is considering for delegation, Jane is the person to whom an activity is being delegated, the level of challenge in sailing the vessel and the difficulty of the course represent the complexity of the activity being delegated, and the weather represents the environment in which the activity is being conducted (e.g. political or financial).

The delegation option that would best suit scenario 1 is what I call a 'directing' form of delegation. Each one of the tacks being made by the vessel to stay close to the layline represents a short review meeting or check-in that a leader would have to discuss progress and agree the next step. This type of delegation is totally appropriate where the person completing the activity needs to learn how to do it as they progress and needs strong support from the leader. It is also appropriate when the leader feels the need to keep a tight rein over the activity. This may be because it is a sensitive project, the environment is challenging, or there is some doubt about the person's ability to keep on track (e.g. there have been past examples of failing to deliver).

Regardless of the reason, 'directing' keeps the leader more in control of the activity, even though it is still being executed by someone else. Of course, due to the increased number of check-ins, this form of delegation still takes quite a lot of the leader's own time and therefore needs to be carefully considered. While directing is totally appropriate sometimes, if it is used in situations that do not really warrant it, it is often described as 'micro-managing'. If a leader is deliberately choosing a 'directing' approach, it is vital that they explain the reasons why to the person executing the activity. Done well, this can really have a motivational impact on that person.

The delegation option that would best suit scenario 2 is what I call a 'deputising' form of delegation. In this approach, the leader needs to be very clear about what is expected and when it is expected by and then hands over total control to the person executing the activity. Obviously, that person should be comfortable to raise any issues by exception to the leader as the activity is executed, but basically, the leader takes a hands-off approach. This type of delegation is totally appropriate when the person executing the activity has the knowledge and experience to handle it alone. It may also be appropriate when the task is relatively simple and is considered low risk.

Regardless of the reason, 'deputising' takes the least amount of the leader's own time because it is under the complete control of someone else. Of course, this means the leader has little or no control of the activity and may be exposed to risks if the person executing it fails to do so effectively or in a timely manner. While 'deputising' is totally appropriate sometimes, if it is used in situations that do not really warrant it, it could easily be described as 'neglect'. Leaders who hand over control of activities to people who are not ready for them, or when those activities have complexities or risks that are significant, are effectively throwing people into the deep end of the pool and letting them sink. However, done well, this form of delegation demonstrates great trust, respect and empowerment for people and can also be extremely motivational.

The delegation option that would best suit scenario 3 (the in-between scenario) is what I call a 'coaching' form of delegation. In this approach, the leader would arrange intermittent check-ins with the person executing the activity. In these check-ins, the leader might first ask the person how things have progressed to date and what they are planning to do from here. The leader may then make their own observations and suggestions, and together they will agree on the best course of action. This type of delegation is a terrific way to stretch the existing capabilities of a person while still providing support along the way. It is a safe way to bring about the transition from the very intensive 'directing' approach to the completely hands-off approach of 'deputising'.

If leaders appropriately utilise these three forms of delegation, they are highly likely to hit a 'quantum jackpot' by increasing capability, increasing trust and increasing energy in the people they are delegating to. The quantum leap in individual performance that follows can be truly astounding. From the leader's own perspective, utilising these delegation options also means that many more activities can be delegated than would have previously been the case. Even tasks that are highly important and quite complex can still be executed by other people. This then has the effect of making more of the leader's own time available for higher order leadership activities. The leader's own priority matrix begins to look more like that shown in the model below, and the majority of his/her own time is spent in what I call the 'leadership zone'. To be able to implement the quantum leadership activities that I will be discussing in the rest of this book, leaders most definitely need this leadership zone to be as large as possible.

An improved model

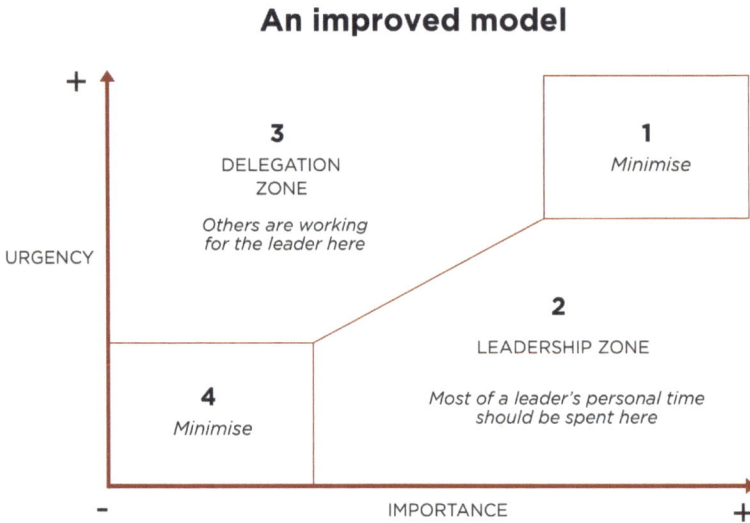

Emotional intelligence

The third foundational quantum leadership capability is derived from the 'with and through other people' part of our leadership definition. Leaders are in the people business! To be successful, leaders need to be able to embrace the diversity in every person with whom they interact and who is in some way affected by their leadership. They need to be able to adapt their approach to suit different people and different situations. Ultimately, they need to be able to provide leadership that takes full advantage of the capabilities people already have and inspires them to unlock their full potential to achieve things way beyond what they already have.

All of this points to the importance of a leader's emotional intelligence. This is a term that to most leaders will already be familiar. There are now libraries full of books and millions of websites that discuss the topic of emotional intelligence in some way. Like many leadership related topics that are widely discussed, it is also a concept that can become too complicated for busy organisational leaders. My simple description of emotional intelligence is that it comprises three key elements.

Practical emotional intelligence

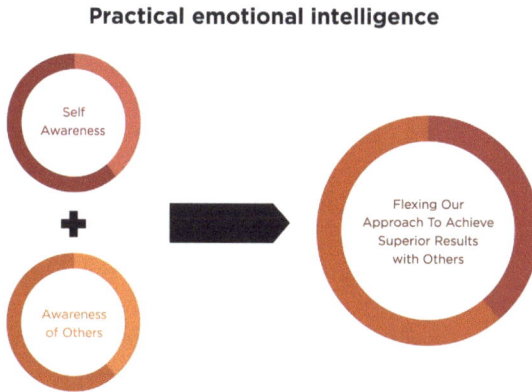

The first element is self-awareness, which in this context is a leader's awareness of their own style, how they like to operate, how they are perceived by others, their strengths, and their weaknesses or challenges when it comes to relating to other people. The second element is awareness of others, which in this context is a leader's ability to understand all of the same things about the person or people with whom they are interacting or who is/are affected by their leadership. The third element, and most important in my opinion, is a leader's ability to flex (or adapt) their approach to achieve a superior result with the person or people with whom they are interacting.

Many leaders, over the course of their careers, are likely to have participated in some form of personality profiling. This may have been as part of a leadership or team development program, or possibly as part of an application process for a job. There are many tools that organisations commonly utilise for this kind of profiling. Some of the most common include Myers Briggs Type Indicator (MBTI), DISC, Herman Brain Dominance Index (HBDI) and Enneagram, but there are literally hundreds of different tools that I have come across in my coaching career. It is fair to say that most of these are really quite excellent tools and can produce truly insightful profiles of the individual completing them.

The practical issue with most of these tests, though, is that they require an individual to complete a battery of questions before they are able to produce a report on that person's profile. This means that they are fine to use for the 'self-awareness' component of emotional intelligence, but they really do not help with the 'awareness of others' element, unless those other people have also answered the battery of questions and had their own profile reported and shared. This is of no use for a leader's practical, day-to-day emotional intelligence, because a leader cannot ask everyone they interact with to answer a bunch of questions so that they can profile them!

I have also met a lot of people who complete some kind of personality profile, receive their profile report, and happily label themselves as a [however the tool describes their particular style], and then do absolutely nothing with it. A memorable example was during a workshop I was running in 2005 when a man in the cohort proudly announced to everyone that he had already been profiled 10 years earlier and knew that he was an ISTJ (from the MBTI profile). I said that was great and asked him to explain to those who were not familiar with that tool what an ISTJ was. He replied, 'Well I know that "I" is for introvert, and I'm definitely an introvert because I find people quite de-energising to deal with. I can't remember what the other letters are all about, but I'm definitely an ISTJ!' I then asked him how knowing that he was an ISTJ had helped him over the years. He looked at me with a strange expression on his face and asked what I meant. I said, 'Well, how have you used that information to get better results with people?' He replied, 'Well, if people know I'm an ISTJ, they should know what they need to do to get a better result with me!'

This was a very good example of the important difference between profiling and emotional intelligence. In a leadership context, emotional intelligence is all about leaders taking the responsibility to try different approaches that will get better results with other people. It is absolutely not about expecting other people to change their approach to suit them. In fact, I describe that as the opposite of emotional intelligence! Yes, it is great when a leader comes across someone who is able to adapt their approach to suit the leader, but that is a reflection of that person's emotional intelligence, not the leader's.

A simple and practical emotional intelligence model

In order to address these problems with traditional personality profiling tools, my colleagues and I at Executive Central developed an emotional intelligence framework that enables leaders to successfully address all three elements of the simplified emotional intelligence model that we have already discussed — self-awareness, awareness of others and flexing — to achieve superior results. We call this model the Executive Central Operating Styles model, or ECOS for short (all good models need a nice acronym!)

The ECOS model is designed to be a tool that leaders can easily use on a day-to-day basis to help them achieve superior results with any other person with whom they might interact. It does not require anyone to answer a battery of questions. I like to describe it as a 'mud map' in that it is not intended to deliver an absolutely perfect, detailed profile of any individual. It is, however, intended to help leaders develop an indicative profile of any person, which can be updated and refined as the leader has further interactions with that person. With this profile, the leader can identify strategies that are likely to work well when interacting with that person and, importantly, avoid dealing with that person in any way that is highly likely to deliver poor outcomes.

The fundamental concept behind the ECOS model is the idea that when it comes to interacting with others, human beings are just like an antenna that both transmits and receives. All people transmit from themselves out to the world using different forms of transmission behaviour. These include speaking, body language, facial expressions, gestures, actions (e.g. the way a leader walks down a hallway transmits a message), writing, emailing, texting, etc. Equally, all people receive in to themselves from the world through different forms of reception behaviour. These include the five senses of sight (observing), sound (listening), touch, taste and smell. Some people might even be described as having some sort of a sixth sense through their intuition or their ability to pick up on the 'vibe' of a situation.

While every person both transmits and receives, how they transmit and receive varies. If we consider transmission behaviour, some people can be said to transmit on higher power. These people tend to be quite talkative, speak with higher volume and pace, and they are quite expressive, using lots of gestures and facial expressions. They are most likely be quite active and appear energetic. Very importantly, these people tend to speak while they think, often giving listeners a running dialogue of their thought processes. An indicator of higher-power transmission is when someone will tend to jump straight in with a response to a question without hesitation.

On the other end of the transmission spectrum, some people can be said to transmit on lower power. These people tend to be less talkative, speak with lower volume and pace, and use fewer expressive

gestures and facial expressions. They tend to be quite deliberate and careful in their actions. These people are quite considered in the way they transmit and, very importantly, will tend to think before they speak. An indicator of lower-power transmission is when someone will give a silent pause before they say anything in response to a question.

Both higher and lower power transmission behaviours are very common and are typically quite easy to identify. As we will discuss shortly, there are pros and cons that come with either style of transmission, so there is most definitely no right or wrong, just difference. Therefore, to use the ECOS model, the first step for a leader to take is to determine whether they perceive a person to have higher-power or lower-power transmission.

There is also a spectrum when it comes to reception behaviour. Some people can be described as having broadband reception. This means that they tend to receive many different things at the same time. For example, people with broadband reception not only hear what someone has said, they also pick up on body language, emotions, feelings, subtleties, messages between the lines, etc. Equally, when they are looking at something, they do not notice just that one thing, they notice other things around it. It is as if they are a sponge that sucks in everything that is going on around them.

Other people can be described as having focused reception. This means that they tend to concentrate very strongly on one thing at a time and while they are focused on that one thing, they are very strongly receiving everything about that one thing. However, they are

less likely to be receiving anything else. For example, when a person with focused reception is focusing on solving a problem, they will not notice anything other than factors associated with that problem. When their attention moves to be focused on a person, then they are totally focused on that person and will receive everything about that person but will not notice anything else. It is as if they have a magnifying glass over whatever they are currently focusing on.

Both broadband and focused reception behaviours are very common. Identifying people at either end of the reception spectrum can sometimes be a little more challenging and requires a bit of practise. As a reasonable rule of thumb, broadband reception people tend to be more people-oriented, concerned about feelings and emotion, and will make decisions with their heart, while focused reception people tend to be more task-oriented, concerned about facts and concrete evidence, and make decisions with their head.

Again, there are pros and cons that come with either style of reception, so there is most definitely no right or wrong, just difference. Therefore, to use the ECOS model, the second step for a leader to take is to determine whether they would perceive a person to have broadband or focused reception.

The ECOS model takes these two dimensions of behaviour — transmission and reception — and compares the combination of them in the individual whose style is being profiled. This creates a quadrant model as shown in the diagram below:

Operating Styles

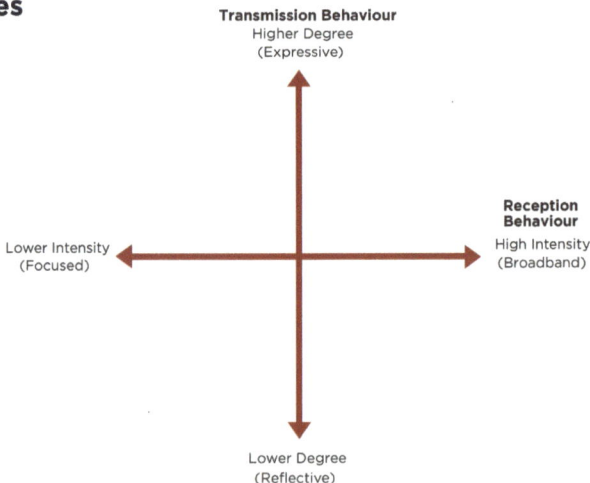

Transmission Behaviour
Higher Degree
(Expressive)

Reception Behaviour
High Intensity
(Broadband)

Lower Intensity
(Focused)

Lower Degree
(Reflective)

Using this basic construct, it is very easy for leaders to plot themselves and anyone else with whom they interact. Once an initial plot has been established, leaders can then consider the more detailed description of the style that corresponds to each of the quadrants and decide if they have themselves and/or each person they are considering in the correct profile.

Introducing the six operating styles

While there are only four quadrants in the model shown above, there are actually six operating styles that we have identified, all of which are commonly found throughout organisations. We draw them on the ECOS model as follows:

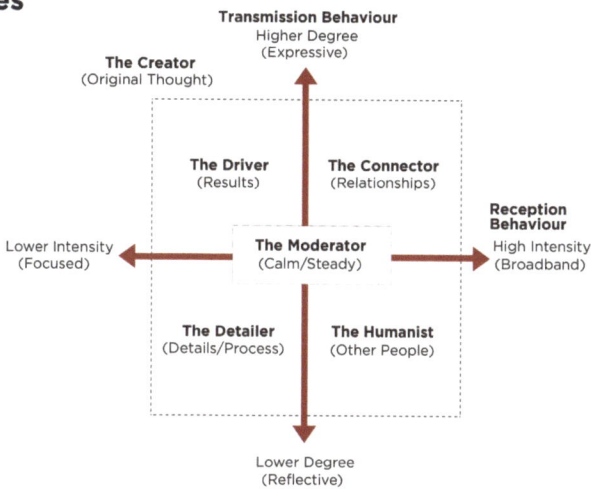

The connector

People who are determined to have both higher-power transmission and high-intensity, broadband reception have an operating style that we call the connector. The pinnacle need (i.e. the thing that is most important) of connectors revolves around the status of their relationship with whomever they are dealing, and they will do what is required to ensure the relationship is healthy. Connectors like to be liked, trusted and respected, and they like to like, trust and respect anyone they

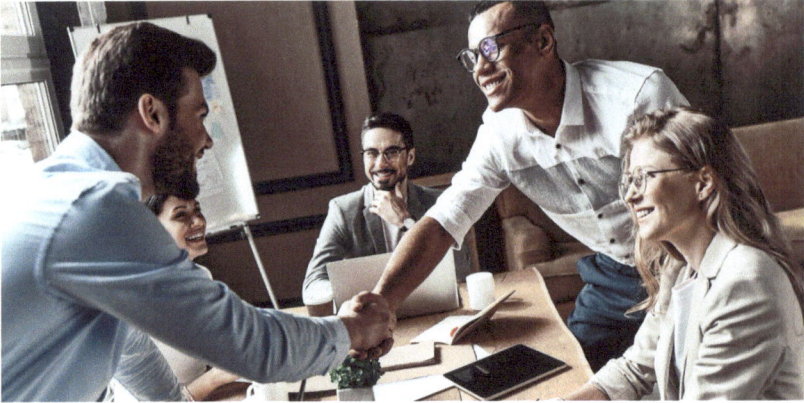

are dealing with. In order to build quality relationships, they will tend to be quite social, conversational people and they like to be involved in activities that involve other people. Connectors will tend to prefer 'big picture' concepts and thoroughly enjoy 'brainstorming', both for its creative and social elements.

The driver

People who are determined to have higher-power transmission and low-intensity, focused reception have an operating style that we call the driver. The pinnacle need of drivers revolves around the achievement of results. Drivers need to feel that results are being achieved, or at least progress is being made towards results, and they will do what is required to ensure this is the case. Drivers communicate clearly, concisely and even commandingly in order to achieve results. They are quite prepared to roll up their sleeves and be hands-on if that is what is required to achieve the result. Drivers will not hesitate to

make decisions, solve problems and take action to ensure progress is happening, and they do not just talk about results, they measure results. Drivers will often be surrounded by graphs, project plans, photographs, even trophies — anything that provides evidence that results have been achieved.

The detailer

People who are determined to have lower-power transmission and low-intensity, focused reception have an operating style that we call the detailer. The pinnacle need of detailers revolves around ensuring that details are not missed so that any activity is reliable, repeatable and predictable. Detailers like to de-risk anything they are doing by conducting detailed research and analysis to ensure they have all available information before proceeding. In order to concentrate on these detailed activities, they tend to prefer to work on their own or in quieter environments. Detailers are very good at turning concepts into reality by developing detailed processes and considering all of the possibilities concerning those concepts.

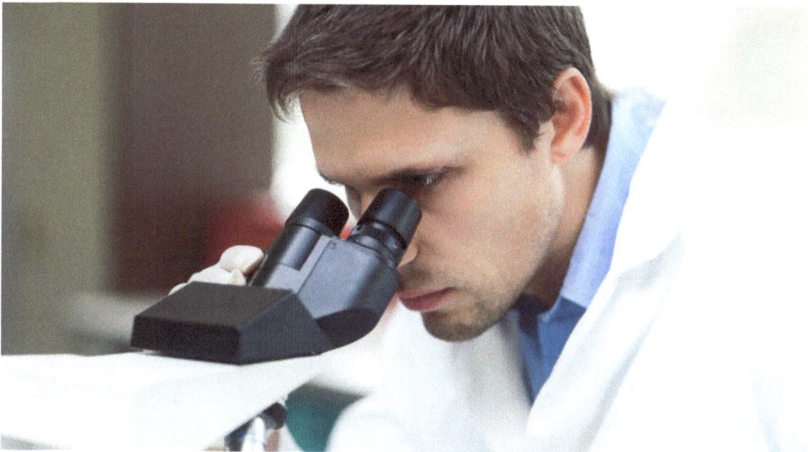

The humanist

People who are determined to have lower-power transmission and high-intensity, broadband reception have an operating style that we call the humanist. The pinnacle need of humanists revolves around the wellbeing of other people. Humanists are very tuned in to what is happening for other people. They are very concerned that any decision is fair (to other people), has positive impacts (on other people), and that those making the decision have properly consulted (with other

people). Humanists are very aware of the feelings of other people, and their own emotions can often mirror the prevailing emotions of those around them. If other people are happy, humanists are happy. If other people are stressed, humanists are stressed, and so on. Humanists are very intuitive when it comes to other people and will often pick up aspects of a person's behaviour or feelings that others would not.

Outside of the styles that reside in the four main quadrants of the ECOS model, there are two other styles that do not specifically sit in any one quadrant.

The moderator

People who are determined to have moderate transmission and moderate intensity reception have an operating style that we call the moderator. Moderators have a degree of flexibility in both their transmission and reception behaviours, but they will never show extremes of any behaviour. Therefore, someone is not really a moderator unless they would be described as always calm and steady. A moderator's pinnacle need revolves around balance. They are happy when decisions are made in a balanced way, people behave in a balanced way, and the atmosphere around them is balanced and calm. Moderators tend to make very good moderators of meetings, or chairs of boards or committees because they can keep things calm and bring issues to a balanced conclusion. They also tend to be able to get on reasonably well with all types of people, because they are unlikely to behave themselves in a strong enough way to annoy anyone.

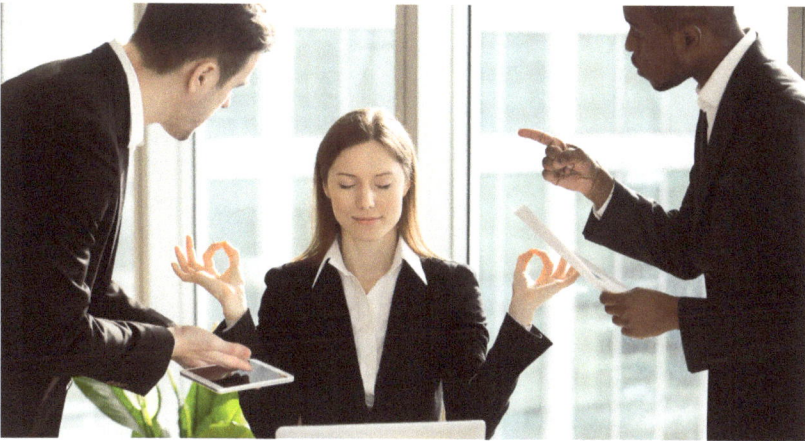

The creator

People who are determined to display behaviour that can be at the extremes of both ends of the transmission and reception spectrums have an operating style that we call the creator. The pinnacle need of creators revolves around original thought — the big idea! Creators tend to always have a big idea on the go at any one time, and behaviourally they will go wherever they feel they need to, in the extreme, to support their current big idea. This means that on any one day, creators could be showing extreme versions of connector, driver, detailer or humanist behaviour at different times throughout that day. Thus, they would often be described as behaving unpredictably. Creators often see things that others cannot. They view the world, and the issues and opportunities in it, through a different lens to most other people. This makes them capable of high levels of idea generation and creative problem solving.

Clouds of behaviour

While the styles described above can provide an excellent insight into how any individual likes to operate, obviously they do not tell us everything about a person. No human being is ever just a single point on a model like this. Indeed, every person can display attributes at times of any of these operating styles. Clearly, though, every person will have a style where they are most comfortable and that is what we are really trying to identify.

We describe people as typically having a 'cloud of behaviour'. For the four main quadrant styles, this cloud will tend to cover their own preferred operating style and the two neighbouring quadrants. When a person is operating in normal, relaxed conditions, their behaviour will typically be spread anywhere within this cloud, and that will seem quite normal to anyone who knows them. For example, a connector's cloud would look something like this:

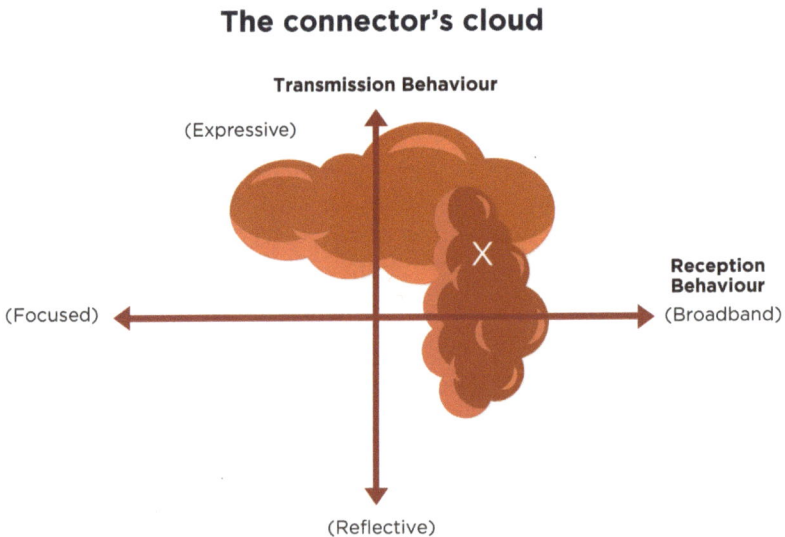

The connector's cloud

Transmission Behaviour

(Expressive)

(Focused)

Reception Behaviour

(Broadband)

(Reflective)

For connectors who are operating in a normal, relaxed environment, it is not unusual for them to display some characteristics of driver, humanist, or moderator behaviour. It is important to note that this does not mean that connectors cannot do detailed tasks, they can and often do. What it means is that they are least comfortable in the detailer space and will want to get out of that mode as quickly as they can. An extended period operating in the detailer space will most likely be highly de-energising for a connector.

The same type of cloud shape applies to each of the other main quadrant styles — drivers, detailers and humanists — and they will commonly display traits of the neighbouring styles under normal, relaxed conditions. Equally, they are likely to find that the style diagonally opposite their preferred style is the least comfortable for them to be in. Moderators may display certain attributes of any of the four main quadrant styles when operating under such conditions but will always be centred on calm and steady behaviour. Creators tend to behave in the extremes of the four main quadrant styles as a normal part of their behaviour. The one thing creators are highly unlikely to ever be is calm and steady. So, it is fair to say that moderators are the equivalent of the diagonal opposite of creators.

Self-awareness in leaders

Being able to identify their own operating styles using the ECOS model is one way for leaders to increase their levels of self-awareness. This includes being aware of the great strengths that come with their style and being aware of the consequences of overplaying the strengths of their style. I will explain this in the context of the ECOS model and the clouds of behaviour.

While everyone has a 'cloud of behaviour' when they are operating in a normal, relaxed environment, this changes when they are operating in a stressed environment. When I say a 'stressed environment', I mean that there is something happening in a leader's environment that they perceive as some kind of threat. Threats can be anything from time pressures, to financial pressures, to people issues and many more things. Put simply, when leaders perceive any threat in their environment, they will change their behaviour to try to protect themselves from that threat. This usually means they will be operating in a way that most suits their own preferences where they are most comfortable.

Under stress, therefore, the cloud of behaviour will tend to disappear, leaving the leader in the centre of gravity of their own operating style; if anything, they will actually move more strongly into that operating style. I have used the connector style as an example again over the page:

The connector under stress

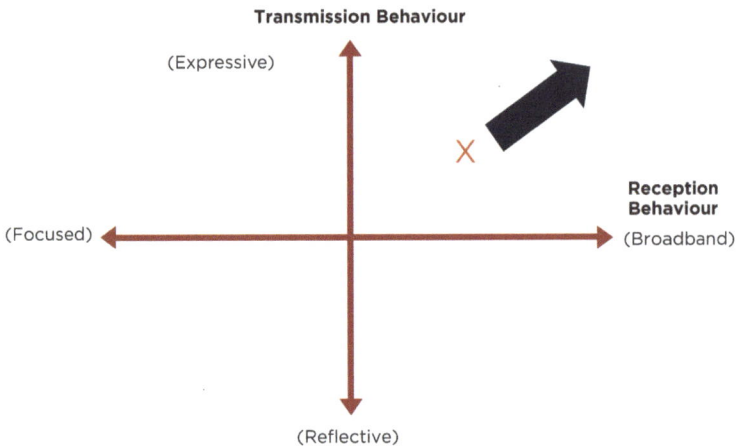

Transmission Behaviour

(Expressive)

X

Reception Behaviour

(Focused)

(Broadband)

(Reflective)

The exact same thing happens to drivers, detailers and humanists when they operate under stress, only their behaviour will move more strongly out to the extremes of their own style. In the case of moderators operating under stress, their cloud also disappears, but they will stay sitting right in the crosshairs of the model, not showing transmission or reception behaviour in any direction much at all. Creators are different. Under stress, their clouds continue to expand out into the extremes of the model.

When operating in this stressed way and overplaying their strengths, there are many possible consequences that can result for leaders. I will attempt to briefly describe the most common consequences that my colleagues and I come across in our coaching.

Stress reactions and consequences of overplaying strengths

Detailers operating under stress tend to overdo their need for detail and their desire to de-risk things. This will tend to have a braking or stopping effect on the progress of any activity, which can result in deadlines being missed or pressure being put on other activities and other people to keep things on track. Probably the most common example of this is 'analysis paralysis', where the detailer keeps seeking more and more data before making a decision or finishing an activity. Detailers overplaying their strengths can also become inflexible, unwilling to deviate from the standard process, policy or convention, even when they are clearly not working. Finally, because of their

preference for quieter working environments which allow them to concentrate, detailers tend to isolate themselves when under stress, which can give the incorrect impression that they are anti-social or not a team player.

Humanists operating under stress tend to overdo their desire for everyone to be happy and/or treated fairly. If they then perceive that this is not the case, humanists tend to take on the worries of everyone, which can be exhausting for them. Humanists can become quite 'wounded' on behalf of other people and when wounded, they may stay wounded for a long time, struggling to move past something that has been a negative experience. The overarching impact that humanists can have when they are operating under stress is to fail to achieve the results they are being asked to deliver. This is primarily due to the fact that they are spending so much time worrying about other people and their issues, that they fail to focus on their own responsibilities or areas of influence to the extent that they should.

Drivers operating under stress tend to overdo their need to make things happen, drive progress and get results. Typically, the consequences of them doing this result in some form of unintended negative impact on other people. Their communication may be perceived as overbearing, harsh, cutting, unfeeling, blunt, or rude, causing a negative impact on their relationship with other people. Drivers may become overly focused on taking action, jumping at the first option available to ensure something is happening, even though other options might have delivered better results. They may become too hands-on, taking over from others whose job it actually is to complete the task. They may also fail to listen to the full story being told by another person, jumping in and assuming they know enough to make a decision, solve the problem, or take action.

Connectors operating under stress tend to overdo their desire to get involved in things with other people. They may struggle to say no to activities for fear of missing out on the social opportunities they might present. This tends to manifest as them having more things on their plate than they can possibly handle, which leads to certain things, usually the finer details, slipping through the cracks. When overplaying their strengths, connectors may skim across the details of things that really require more attention, they may over-trust that others have done what they have said they will do, and they may fail to think ahead or anticipate things beyond the immediate future. Connectors may also find it hard to address difficult people-related issues or make difficult decisions when under stress for fear that doing so may negatively impact the way people regard them or their long-term relationships with those people.

Moderators operating under stress will tend to overdo the calmness and steadiness that they normally show. When this calmness and steadiness is taken to the extreme, it can come across to other people as apathy, a lack of enthusiasm, or a general lack of energy. Moderators operating under stress can appear to be 'sitting on the fence' around pressing issues, because they appear not to be giving those matters an appropriate sense of urgency, or they are do not appear to have strong opinions on the subject in any direction. Moderators who are overplaying their strengths can also appear to lack 'gravitas' or 'presence', tending to portray a somewhat 'bland' image.

Creators operating under stress can potentially be displaying any of the strength-overplayed issues of other styles, with the exception of the moderator, because their already extreme variations in transmission

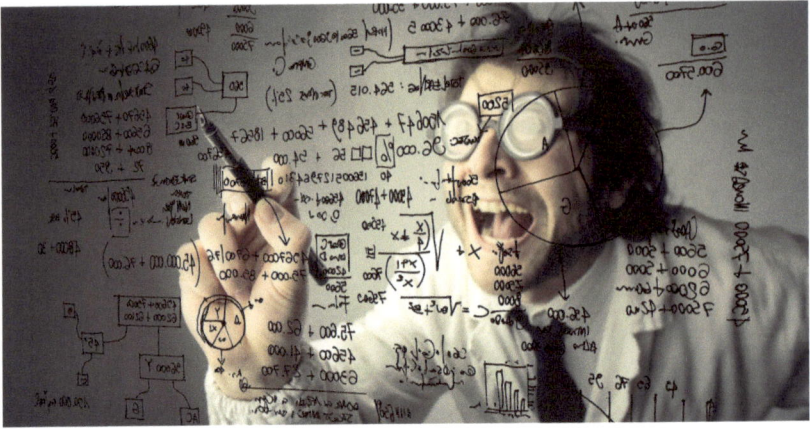

and reception behaviour are magnified even further. Apart from any of these issues, creators who are overplaying their strengths are often seen by others as a major distraction, constantly coming up with new ideas before everyone else has had a chance to understand/digest/execute on any of the previous ideas. Because their behaviour can vary so unpredictably, creators can also lose the trust of other people, who may find it easier to just avoid dealing with them rather than taking the risk that they might strike them on a 'bad day'.

Leaders can use the ECOS model to enhance their own self-awareness and to coach other people to be more self-aware. Helping other people to identify their own operating styles and to be aware of the strengths that style brings and the consequences that can occur when those strengths are overplayed is a simple and effective way to help them on their way to increased emotional intelligence. However, awareness of self and awareness of others does not make someone emotionally intelligent. It is what they do with this information that really counts.

Flexing behaviour for superior results

The key to leaders being emotionally intelligent is their ability to flex or adapt their own behaviour to achieve superior results with other people, once they have accurately profiled the operating styles of themselves and those other people with whom they are interacting.

Flexing does not mean that leaders need to change who they are. A very common mistake is for leaders to think that because a person is a particular style, then the only way to work well with them is to try to mimic that style. This never works because it is not genuine and it is forcing the leaders who try to do this to behave in a way that is not comfortable for them.

To describe flexing, I like to suggest that leaders imagine a spring which, at one end, is anchored at the centre of their preferred operating style. That spring can be stretched in different directions but because it is anchored it will always remain grounded in the preferred operating style. When leaders are flexing, they may stretch their behaviour in different directions (something everyone is capable of doing) but their behaviour will always remain grounded in their preferred operating style.

Another more scientific analogy that really gets to the heart of what flexing is all about is Newton's third law. This law states that 'For every action there is an equal and opposite reaction'. Sir Isaac Newton applied this law to forces in nature, but I am going to apply it to behaviour of humans. Basically, for every flex of behaviour a leader makes, they are likely to get an equal and opposite flex of behaviour from the other person with whom they are interacting.

As an example, let's consider leaders who have higher intensity, broadband reception (humanist or connector) who are trying to get a better result when dealing with people who have low-intensity, focused reception (detailer or driver). If those leaders could slightly move their behaviour towards the left of the model, then it is highly likely the other person will flex their behaviour to the right of the model towards them. This would mean that they would meet somewhere in the middle of their two styles, where they would both most likely be quite comfortable. See diagram below:

How do you need to flex?

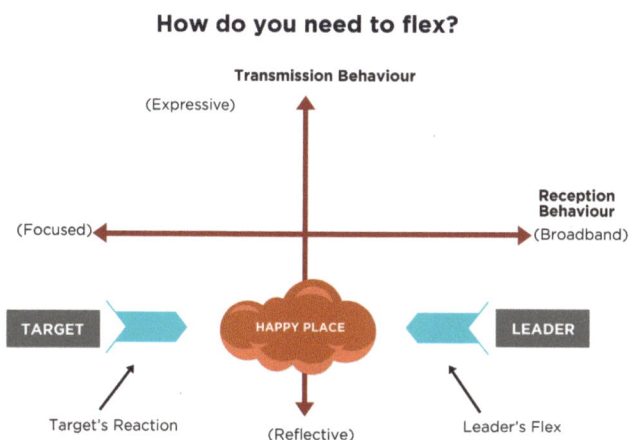

61

In this case, using the construct of the ECOS model as a guide, to make a small flex to the left, leaders who are humanists or connectors need to be slightly turning down the broadband nature of their reception to be more focused than they might normally be. I will discuss options for how this type of flex can be achieved shortly. In return, the detailers or drivers they are dealing with are likely to broaden their reception and pay a little more attention to things other than the specific issue at hand. The result is that both people end up feeling more comfortable dealing with each other.

Leaders who have lower intensity, focused reception (drivers and detailers) who are trying to get better results with people who have high intensity, broadband reception (connectors and humanists) need to flex their behaviour slightly to the right on the model by broadening their reception, in order to get the opposite reaction from the people they are dealing with, and to make the interaction more comfortable for both of them.

The same principle applies to flexing behaviour along the vertical transmission behaviour access. Leaders who have high transmission (connectors and drivers) will need to slightly turn down their transmission behaviour to get a better result with people who have lower transmission (humanists and detailers). By turning down their transmission slightly, they will like get a reaction where the other party turns up their transmission and they meet in the middle. This is comfortable for both parties.

How do you need to flex?

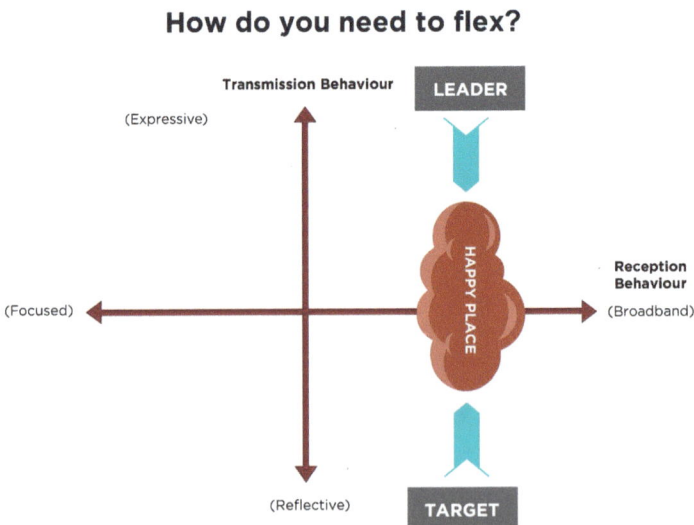

If leaders have one of the lower transmission styles (humanist or detailer), they will need to turn up their transmission behaviour to transmit slightly more than they normally would, when dealing with someone from one of the higher transmission styles (driver or connector). In return, they will likely see that the higher transmission person slightly turns down their transmission so that they meet in the middle and it is comfortable for both of them.

Unfortunately, Newton's third law also works when leaders move their behaviour away from the style of the people they are interacting with. For example, if leaders find interacting with certain people particularly challenging or stressful, they may demonstrate their stress reaction and move their behaviour very strongly into the extremities of their preferred operating style. In return, they are likely to get the equal and opposite reaction from the person with whom they are interacting, which is that person's stress reaction. The end result is that their behaviours are poles apart and it will be extremely uncomfortable for them to deal with each other.

Stress reactions

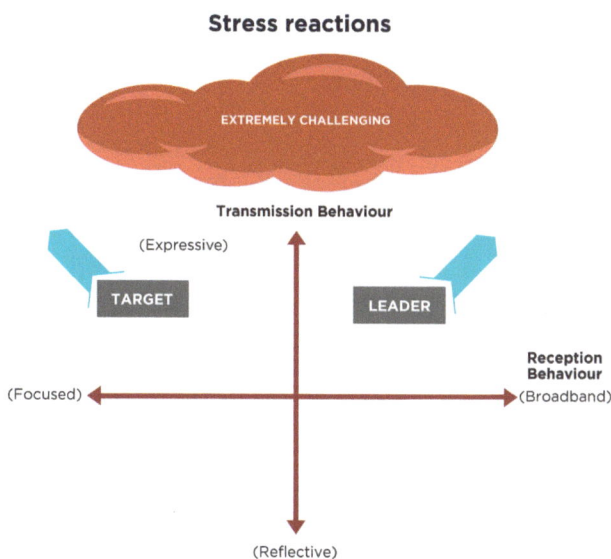

This is another reason why leaders need to be extremely conscious of how they are behaving and the impact it is having on those with whom they are interacting. If leaders are generating a stress reaction in other people because of the way they are behaving themselves, then they most certainly will not be creating an environment where quantum leaps in performance at any level are possible.

Natural tensions – dealing with the diagonal

Once leaders have profiled themselves and the people with whom they are interacting, if it turns out that their own operating style is the diagonal opposite to another person's operating style, this is what I call a 'natural tension'. The operating styles that are diagonally opposite each other on the ECOS model are the most unlike each other because they differ in both transmission and reception behaviour. (Note: I define the moderator as being the diagonal opposite of the creator as well.) It is also interesting to note that whenever someone is overplaying their strengths under stress, the first issues they tend to encounter relate very strongly to the style that is diagonally opposite them, i.e. connectors start missing details, drivers start creating people issues, humanists start failing to deliver results, detailers withdraw from people, moderators lack passion and urgency, creators are completely unpredictable.

It is still vitally important for leaders to flex their behaviour to get a better result with anyone with a diagonally opposite operating style to their own. However, this is one case where I definitely do not recommend trying to flex directly towards that person. In other words, it is not a good idea to try to flex diagonally. The reason I do not recommend this is because it requires leaders to be flexing both transmission and reception behaviour at the same time to achieve the diagonal flex. This starts to require leaders to be changing too many things about their normal behaviour and it is highly unlikely to feel comfortable or genuine for them.

My suggested strategy for dealing with diagonally opposite operating styles is to decide on one of the 'neutral corners' and try to make one strong flex (of either transmission or reception behaviour) to get into that neutral corner. The likely reaction will be that the other person will also move to that neutral corner. Even if they do not, it is likely that the chances of a productive interaction with that person will be much higher than if no flex was attempted and the 'natural tension' was allowed to dominate the interaction.

Specific flexing strategies

The beauty of the ECOS model is that when it comes to flexing strategies there are really only four categories of possible behavioural flexes and most people will only ever need to worry about two of them.

Dealing with natural tensions

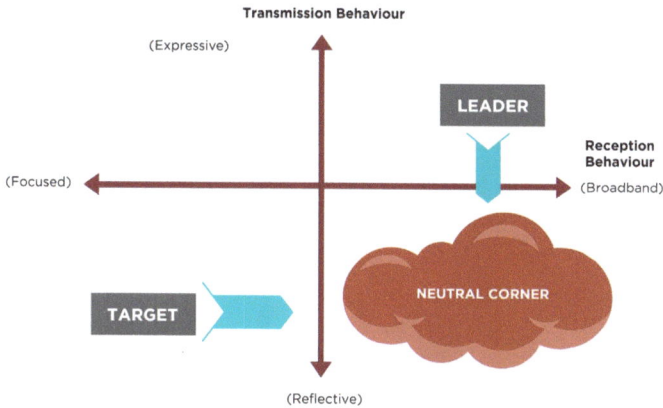

These four categories are:

1. Broadening reception behaviour
2. Focusing reception behaviour
3. Decreasing transmission behaviour
4. Increasing transmission behaviour.

For each of these, there are literally hundreds of strategies that can be used to make the required flex. I am going to focus on simple strategies that in my experience have worked very effectively for leaders whom I have coached over the years. The idea is to pick just one of these suggestions and focus on executing it well to test if it has the desired effect. If that strategy does not work, another strategy can be selected for the next interaction with that person to see if that works. Through a process of testing and refining, leaders can determine what works with each person with whom they interact.

Once I have outlined these ideas for each specific flex, I will then share a technique that I have come to describe as the 'universal flex', which is a fantastic option for leaders to use in situations where they have not been able to decide on a specific flexing strategy for the person or people with whom they are interacting.

Broadening reception behaviour

The goal here is to try to signal to the other party that you are **interested in what they are saying** and really want to **understand what they think**. You may just find that you also benefit from this by understanding more than you might have otherwise!

Some suggestions on how leaders can achieve this flex include:

- Asking follow-up or qualifying questions and really listening to their answers
- Fully focusing on the other person and not thinking ahead while they are speaking
- Summarising what they have said to ensure both accurate comprehension and to signal that they have been truly listened to
- Ensuring your body language is 'open' and suggesting you are 'welcoming' what they have got to say
- Smiling and nodding a lot to let them know that their thoughts and suggestions are appreciated
- Asking their opinions before suggesting your own opinion
- Making questions as open as possible to invite more information (i.e. What?, Where?, When?, How?, Why?)

Focusing reception behaviour

The goal here is to try to signal to the other party that you are **very calm and unemotional** and that you are purely **interested in receiving the facts of the situation.**

Some suggestions on how you might achieve this include:

- Using 'imagery' to prepare before the meeting e.g. putting on an invisible 'suit of armour' to provide protection from any arrows fired in your direction, or energizing an invisible protective force-field and creating a safe space from which to calmly observe the outside world. (Note: This might sound a bit whacky at first but trust me, this kind of mental imagery can really help!)
- Fully focusing on the words that are being spoken, not the way they are speaking them
- Summarising what has been heard (calmly) to ensure the facts

are correct, to overcome any incorrect impressions they may have given, and to show control

- Ensuring body language is 'neutral' and suggesting confidence and control

- Taking notes, which indicates a desire to get the facts and details correct and that what they are saying is considered important and worthy of remembering

- Taking notes to reduce the amount of time spent looking at the other party and thus reducing the visual stimulus you are receiving

- Using more 'closed' questions to confirm facts and eliminate any unnecessary additional information (i.e. questions that can be answered yes or no).

Decreasing transmission behaviour

The goal here is to try to signal to the other party that you are **interested in what they have to say and that their opinions are worth listening to.**

Some suggestions on how you might achieve this include:

- Speaking less often and with less volume and speed

- Not interrupting or 'speaking over' them until they have finished what they have said

- Avoiding 'filling in' the silent pauses they might leave with your own words

- Allowing them time to think through what they want to say and letting them be the one to break the silence (this takes a lot of patience and practice)

- Ensuring body language is 'neutral' and suggesting you are 'welcoming' what they have got to say

- Nodding and maintaining eye contact with the other person/ people to let them know that you are engaged in the conversation and interested in listening to them

- Avoiding being distracted by things outside the conversation (e.g. other people, emails, texts, phone calls) — this requires practising complete concentration

- Trying to speak for less than 50 per cent of the time in the conversation.

Increasing transmission behaviour

The goal here is to try to signal to the other party that **you do have something to say and have opinions that are worth listening to**. You also want to indicate that **you are engaged** in the conversation.

Some suggestions on how you might achieve this include:

- Speaking up more often and with more volume and speed
- Avoiding being interrupted or 'spoken over' until you have finished speaking e.g. use phrases like 'Hang on, just let me finish this point before it jumps out of my head and I forget it' or 'Hold on a sec, just let me finish as I think this point is really worth considering'
- Not allowing the conversation to 'move on' until you are ready to let it do so, e.g. ask for a moment to think about what is being suggested and its implications (this is a great way to show you are engaged in the conversation even though you may not have said much up to this point)
- Ensuring body language is 'open' and 'leaning in' to the conversation to suggest you are fully engaged
- Nodding and maintaining eye contact with the other person/ people to let them know that you are engaged in the conversation (even if you are not saying anything)
- If you have nothing to add, say 'I've got nothing to add' rather than remaining silent (which can give the incorrect impression of disengagement).

The universal flex — funnelling

Funnelling is a technique whereby one person (let's call them the questioner) asks an initial question of another person about whatever the topic of their conversation is. The questioner listens carefully to the other person's answer to that first question, and then asks another question about something the other person said in that answer. The other person will then answer the second question, and the questioner will then ask another question about something in

Universal flex - funnelling

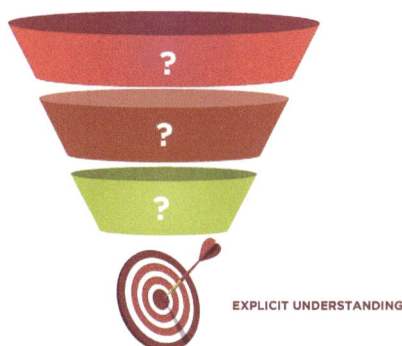

EXPLICIT UNDERSTANDING

that second answer. This process can continue until the questioner has an explicit understanding of what the other person is saying and why they are saying it. I call this 'funnelling' because each follow-up question is delving deeper into the funnel to gain more detailed facts and information.

This all sounds fairly simple, doesn't it? I can assure you, however, that it is a technique that requires quite a lot of concentration and practise if you are to become highly proficient in it. While it might sound as though funnelling is all about questioning, the truth is it is far more about quality listening. To be able to ask appropriate follow-up questions, the questioner needs to be able to listen with their full concentration to the answers the other person is giving. My observation is that funnelling, and more specifically, listening, is not something that is currently being done very well in many parts of society, and I certainly include many organisations in that statement.

There are two very common practices, which are far more common than funnelling, that I think everyone should be very aware of because we all do them from time to time (some more than others) and they are bad habits that lead to less than optimal outcomes in communication.

The first is where a person might ask a couple of questions but they listen to the answers only until the point where the other person says something that reminds them of their own story or experience, and then they jump straight in and start telling their own story. For example, the conversation might go something like this:

Q. How was your weekend?

A. Pretty good thanks.

Q. What did you get up to?

A. We went down to the Gold Coast to visit my parents.

Q. Oh! We love the Gold Coast. We went there for a four-week holiday over Christmas and the kids absolutely loved the surf and sand. We are thinking we'd love to buy a place there some day …

I call this practice 'funnel-chopping'. The questioner chops off the other person's story, stops listening to them, and takes over the conversation with their own story. This practice is so common that I think it is fair to say that there is a funnel-chopping pandemic sweeping the world, and its impact, frankly, though not as life-and-death as Covid-19, is extremely negative. When people do not listen in order to understand properly what others are saying and when they dominate with their own views, this poor communication can have devastating effects on individuals, teams, organisations and societies in general.

The second practice is where people think they are doing the right thing by asking a lot of questions, but they are not really listening to the answers they are getting. Even though the questions might be about the same topic, none of them relate in any way to anything the other person says. For example, the conversation might go something like this:

Q. What is your favourite kind of vacation?

A. I love going on cruises.

Q. When do you typically go on vacation?

A. I prefer summer.

Q. How long is your typical vacation?

A. About two weeks.

Q. Who do you go on vacation with?

A. My wife and kids.

After a short while, the other person is thinking 'Why are you asking me so many questions about my vacations?'

I call this practice 'funnel-hopping'. Basically, the questioner is opening up a new funnel with each question but is failing to go down any funnel beyond the first question. This really starts to feel like interrogation after a while and most people will eventually grow very tired of it.

One of the most valuable things about using funnelling is that it delivers a far greater understanding of the facts, for both parties. Getting beneath someone's initial statement and uncovering more specific details gives the questioner far more accurate information to eventually respond to. Having to be more explicit in their responses also makes the other person think more deeply about what they are saying, which results in far better dialogue, decisions, solutions, ideas, etc.

It is in the context of flexing that funnelling also offers tremendous value. This is due to the fact that it is a technique that can achieve any one of the four flexes I outlined earlier. In other words, it is a flex that can potentially work in any situation, regardless of the operating styles of the parties involved. Let me explain.

If the flex I need to achieve is to **broaden my reception behaviour,** funnelling helps me do that because the follow-up questions that I ask show the other person that I am listening to and am interested in what they are saying, more than I might do normally.

If the flex I need to achieve is to **focus my reception behaviour,** funnelling helps me do that by forcing me to focus on what the other person is saying, not how they are saying it, in order to be able to ask appropriate follow-up questions.

If the flex I need to achieve is to **increase my transmission behaviour**, funnelling helps me do that because every time I ask a question, I am giving the other person a verbal cue that I am engaged in the conversation, and I am controlling the direction of the conversation with my questions.

If the flex I need to achieve is to **decrease my transmission behaviour**, funnelling helps me do that because while I am listening carefully to the answers the other person is giving me, I am not transmitting at all and they have more space to transmit themselves.

That is why I call funnelling the 'universal flex'. Regardless of what your style is and what the other person's style is, the chances are it will be helping you make the flex you need to make. Most definitely, if the operating style of the other person is unclear, funnelling is a great fall-back strategy to use until you are in a better position to determine their style. It is a technique in which I strongly suggest every quantum leader needs to become proficient.

CHAPTER 3

Increasing capability

The ability of a leader to increase the capability of individuals, teams or organisations (entities) is one of the key factors required to excite a 'quantum leap' in performance. This begs the question, 'How does a leader increase capability?'

Regardless of which entity's performance leaders are focusing on, when it comes to increasing capability there are two available options they can employ. The first is to build new capability. The second is to unlock capability that is already there but not yet being fully utilised. Without question, if a leader can be successful at either of these the end result will be an increase in capability, which is a 'tick in the box' for the capability factor of the quantum equation.

However, because quantum leadership is all about leadership in quantum environments — which, because of their volatile and disruptive characteristics, require a shorter term, more immediate response — it seems to me that it makes more sense to prioritise unlocking capability that is already there but not yet being fully utilised. This is going to be a faster way to increase capability because leaders are not starting from scratch.

Please do not think that I am in any way suggesting that it is not a leader's responsibility to build new capabilities in individuals, teams and organisations. It absolutely is! That is why every book or article I have ever read about leadership is full of methods designed to build new capabilities in these entities. Indeed, a huge amount of the leadership content my colleagues and I have developed since 2004 has been about helping leaders to build new capabilities in people — individually, in teams, and organisation-wide. But writing another book about things that can be read in any other leadership book is not my goal!

In this chapter, I will focus on leadership methods and approaches that can help to unlock existing capability that is not yet being applied or fully utilised. In other words, we are focusing on unlocking *capability potential*.

Taking a coaching approach

Before we investigate leadership methods that unlock existing capability in individuals, I would like to focus on an overarching skill that quantum leaders need. That is the ability to take a coaching approach to building capability.

What is a coaching approach for quantum leaders? Fundamentally, it is a leadership or learning response specifically tailored to recognise that every individual has unique strengths and development needs, and is operating in a unique context. This approach then focuses on supporting people to apply or try new methods in a way that suits their style and situation, and then to sustain these methods until they become entrenched as habits or norms.

Why coach in a quantum environment?

A leader might well ask the question, 'Why would I use a coaching approach to develop capability, which requires a sustained effort from both myself and the person I'm coaching, in a quantum environment? By definition, this is a volatile environment requiring rapid response and action.'

That is a very good question to ask. I will answer it by first considering what the alternatives to a coaching approach are. Based on the behaviours that my colleagues and I observe of leaders operating in such environments, the most commonly used alternatives are: 1. Just telling people what to do, and 2. Sending them on some kind of training course. Let's look at both of these and consider the impact they have in quantum environments.

Why not just tell them what to do?

Just telling people what to do, or 'directing' them as it might be called, is certainly one option that is available to leaders. Indeed, used at the right time and in the right circumstances, directing is a totally appropriate leadership approach, as I have already discussed in the motivational and developmental delegation methodology in chapter 2 of this book. From a quantum environment perspective, the biggest advantage of this option is that it is fast for the leader and gets things happening quickly.

However, what happens when people have completed what the leader directed them to do? That's right, they will be back asking the leader what to do next. Then again once that next task is done, and again and again and again. So, the biggest issue with over-using a directing approach is that it creates a dependence on the leader.

No matter how good leaders are, they are only individuals and there is only one of them to go around! Invariably, leaders over-using a directing approach eventually become bottlenecks in their organisations. Everyone is depending on them to tell them what to do, which means the leader is essentially responsible for coming up with all the answers and making all the decisions. Who says the leader's opinions, ideas and solutions are going to be the right ones, anyway? This 'command and control' approach to leadership, and the issues that come with it, has been the subject of many leadership books.

However, it is when we consider quantum environments that the pitfalls of over-using a command and control, directive approach to leadership become seriously amplified. If the only people thinking, analysing, problem-solving, decision-making, and action-planning in a quantum environment are individual leaders, then the environment will open up like a black hole and swallow those leaders, and ultimately the organisations they lead as well.

Leaders attempting to use this approach in a quantum environment will find themselves operating completely reactively. There is absolutely no time to do a quality job of some of the 'higher order' requirements of a good leader. Things like strategy, change management, stakeholder engagement, stakeholder management, customer engagement, innovation, and environmental scanning are either completely neglected, or are rushed through and completed at the most basic level. The leader is simply fighting too many fires on too many fronts to ever properly attend to such 'non-urgent' things.

Then there is the impact of a leader who is continually working under stress, probably overplaying their own strengths and preferences, and having a less than ideal impact on everyone they engage with — both at work and outside of work. In chapter 2, I covered the topic of stress in the context of its effect on the quality execution of priorities, and in the context of its impact on interpersonal communication and relationships. In chapter 5 I will discuss stress in the context of its impact on the energy levels of people.

In a quantum environment, if leaders think they will succeed by just telling people what to do, and that approach leads to a significant increase in the levels of stress in the environment, the consequences will eventually become dire for leaders personally, everyone they engage with, and the organisations or parts thereof that they lead.

Why not just send people on training courses?

Sending people on training courses when there is a specific skill that they need to develop is certainly an available option for leaders; based on the statistics on training spend around the world, it is certainly an option that is being widely used. Without doubt, training courses have a place and are an appropriate option in the right circumstances. In a quantum environment, using training courses can be a fast and efficient way to get large numbers of people across any new processes, policies, systems, tools, or technical knowledge that they might need to be able to do their jobs or complete tasks that leaders require of them.

However, the biggest issue with using training courses in isolation in a quantum environment is really the same issue with using them in normal business environments. That is the problem of 'training transfer' — how to actually apply what is taught on training courses in the workplace. In the learning and development industry, it is commonly accepted that less than 10 per cent of everything that is taught on training courses is actually applied in the workplace. That is bad enough in normal conditions, but in a quantum environment, where everything is about people responding and acting quickly, having people failing to apply new knowledge and skills is a calamity!

In 2017, I completed a Master of Professional Studies (Coaching Practice) degree, where one of the subjects of my research was 'the transfer problem' as the issue has become known in learning and development circles. I conducted an extensive academic literature review and found that there have been hundreds of studies completed over the last 50 years or so that have identified myriad reasons why the transfer problem exists. The list of reasons is far too long to cover here, but some of the key reasons include: the training is not specific to an individual's needs or context; training is typically a fixed syllabus of content that is taught 'just in case' participants ever need it; there is no involvement of management in the training and hence no support back in the workplace for its implementation; trainees' learning needs and styles are not identified or catered to; and there is a failure by organisations to measure the return on investment of training interventions.

Very interestingly, most of the academic papers that I read were very good at explaining the reasons why the transfer problem is a reality, but none of them really gave any solutions or alternatives that would solve it. My research also included an extensive academic literature review on coaching and its effectiveness as a development methodology. In short, because of its individually tailored nature, its context-specific focus, and its emphasis on the acquisition and application of new knowledge, coaching was found to be an excellent way to avoid the issues associated with the transfer problem and to deliver outstanding return on investment (ROI). So, as a professional executive coach, you can see how I find it ironic that many organisations' development budgets are dominated by training courses conducted in isolation without any coaching support!

In summary, I am not saying that leaders should never just tell people what to do or should never send people on training courses. What I am saying is that in my experience, these approaches are massively overplayed by leaders and organisations, and they just do not cut it in quantum environments. If leaders use a coaching approach either instead of, or in support of, either of these options, they will go a very long way towards unlocking the capability potential that is locked up within people all around them.

How to unlock individual capability potential by coaching

In order to be able to determine the best leadership response to unlocking the capability potential of any individual, a quantum leader must be able to determine or analyse the following qualities: what capability gaps the individual has (these will need to be developed over the longer term); what capabilities the individual already has and is already utilising (these may be able to be utilised even more — 'low hanging fruit'); and what capabilities the individual already has but is not yet utilising (the capability potential to be unlocked). This can be achieved in a number of ways, but the two approaches I suggest are the fastest and most appropriate in a quantum environment are: 1. Utilising a coaching discovery or needs analysis methodology with the individual directly, and 2. Utilising some form of diagnostic tool to discover and assess capability.

Utilising a coaching discovery methodology

I would like to share with you a very simple but extremely powerful methodology that we use in our coaching at Executive Central to help discover what the coachee's current level of capability is, and where they may have development needs. (Note: development needs are not just things a coachee is not good at, they include things that they might be good at but are not doing very much, if at all.) Most importantly, the methodology also helps the coach and coachee to determine whether it is worthwhile even bothering to address their development needs (i.e. are the impacts of not addressing them big enough to make the effort worthwhile?). Indeed, this discovery methodology is extremely effective regardless of whether we are working with individuals, teams, or entire organisations. The methodology is derived from a theory known as the transtheoretical model of change (or TTM). Our nickname for it is the Happy–Sad–Happy model.

The Happy–Sad–Happy model is comprised of six question/ discussion phases or lines of enquiry. The first four phases could be collectively described as a 'coaching needs analysis' and stages 5 and 6 could be described as 'solution development and action planning'. At each phase the coach (or quantum leader in this case) should focus on asking guiding questions, listening intently to the answers, asking follow-up questions, and listening again to get a complete understanding of what the coachee is saying. The coach may then make any suggestions of their own and explore their relevance with the coachee. (Note: in our coaching methodology, is it absolutely fine for the coach/leader to make their own suggestions based on their observations or experience, but it is vital that this comes after the coachee has shared their thoughts.)

In the following sequence, I will describe each phase and provide some examples of the types of questions that might work well in each phase.

Coaching needs analysis

Phase 1 — Strengths/successes

In this phase, we want to explore what is going well for the coachee, and what has helped make them successful. Example questions for an individual are:

What is going well?

- What went well on the [xyz] assignment?
- What were the best things about your leadership of [name]?
- In thinking about [project or task], what was the best thing about it?

Which of your personal strengths have you been using?

- Tell me how you decided to handle [name]? Why?
- You're known as a great [characteristic], how have you used this?

What would you like to be doing even more of if you could?

- Why do you think this would be a benefit?
- How would it improve your performance?

Example questions for a team or organisation are:

What is going well?

- What has been the secret of the team's success so far?
- Where has this current approach worked well for the team?
- What was the thinking when the team first took this approach?
- What does the team like about doing things the current way?

When the coachee has had the chance to fully explain what they feel is a strength and is going well, the coach/leader can then add their own perceptions of what is going well if they feel the coachee has missed something important. When making suggestions like these, it is vital that the coach then returns to a questioning approach to ensure the coachee understands the suggestion that has been made and has the opportunity to expand on it.

Phase 2 — Concerns or development needs

In this phase, we want to explore what is going less well for the coachee, and what is standing in the way of them being more successful. Example questions for an individual are:

What is not going so well?

- What didn't go so well on the [xyz] assignment?
- What were the worst things about your leadership of [name]?
- In thinking about [project or task], what were the lessons you learned?

Do you see any particular skills you need to develop?

- Give me an example of when this has resulted in a less than ideal outcome.
- How do you think others perceived you in [situation]?
- Can you think of any examples of where you may have overplayed your strengths in the [meeting]?

What would you like to be doing less of, if you could?

- Why do you think this is a problem?
- How would rectifying it improve your performance?

Example questions for a team or organisation are:

What is not going so well?

- What problems is the current approach creating?
- In what situations is the current approach not working well?
- What changes have occurred in the market or the team's operational environment that make the current approach less effective?
- What doesn't the team like about the current approach?
- What skill or knowledge deficiencies make the current approach unworkable?

When the coachee has had the chance to fully explain what they see as concerns or development needs, the coach/leader can then add their own perceptions of what is not going well if they feel the coachee has missed something important. When making suggestions like this, again it is vital that the coach then returns to a questioning approach to ensure the coachee understands the suggestion that has been made and has the opportunity to expand on it.

Phase 3 — Consequences

In this phase, we want to explore the consequences of not addressing the concerns and/or development needs that were identified in phase 2. This is the critical phase! If we are unable to discover any consequences of significance to the coachee, then there will be very little propensity for them to engage and address the issues beyond paying them lip service.

It is important to note that three types of consequences are likely to be discovered:

- Organisational consequences are those that will have an impact on the organisation
- Team consequences are those that have an impact on the team
- Individual consequences are those that have an impact on the individual.

Regardless of the entity being coached (individual, team or organisation), it is likely that these three types of consequences exist. For example, if an individual is being coached and it was identified in phase 2 that they are uncomfortable speaking up in meetings, there are likely to be organisational consequences (e.g. decisions are made without all of the information available and lead to poorer outcomes), team consequences (e.g. lack of debate on decisions or ideas), and individual consequences (e.g. coachee is not respected by team members and manager and misses out on best project opportunities).

While all three of these consequences are important to discover, it is the individual consequences that will have the greatest impact on energising and motivating people to make a change in the way they are doing something. So, if organisational or team consequences are discovered, it is always a good idea to keep digging with further questions to uncover what that means for the individual if the issues are not addressed.

Example questions for this phase are:

If this situation was to go unresolved, what do you think the possible outcome might be?

- What impact might this have on your/our business/career/people/reputation/relationships/clients/financial rewards?
- How do you think this might affect people's perception of you?
- Who would be forced to make a decision to rectify the situation? What might they do?
- Can you allow this to happen?
- Can you recover from such a setback?

When the coachee has had the chance to fully explain what they feel the consequences of not addressing the issues are, the coach/leader can then add their own perceptions of potential consequences if they feel the coachee has missed something important.

Phase 4 — Upsides

In this phase, we want to explore what the upsides or opportunities might be if we could address the concerns and/or development needs that were identified in phase 2. This is also a very important phase. If we can identify upsides and opportunities that could have a major positive impact on the coachee — a kind of light at the end of the tunnel — then there will likely be a stronger propensity for them to engage and address the issues.

In this phase, it is again likely that organisational upsides, team upsides and individual upsides will exist. It will be the individual upsides that generate the greatest energy towards change, so it is important to dig deep with further questions to explore what an organisational or team upside means to the individual(s) involved.

Example questions for this phase are:

If you could successfully demonstrate your ability to address these issues, what do you think that might mean for you?

- What opportunities might present themselves in your business/career/people/reputation/relationships/clients?

- How do you think this might affect people's perception of you?

- Who would see your/our ability more clearly? What might they do?

- What financial rewards might result?

- What other opportunities might there be?

When the coachee has had the chance to fully explain what they think the upsides and opportunities from addressing the development needs are, the coach/leader can then add their own perceptions of potential upsides if they feel the coachee has missed something important.

Coaching solutions and actions

Phase 5 — Solutions

In this phase, we want to explore what potential solutions will address the development needs (identified in phases 1 and 2), avoid the consequences (identified in phase 3), and realise the upsides (identified in phase 4). In a coaching approach, it is important that the coachee is actively involved in designing any solution. If the coach/leader just jumps in and gives what they think the answer is, all that is being developed is a dependence on the coach/leader. So, the best approach here is to again ask first, then suggest.

Example questions for this phase are:

Based on the **explicit needs** *we've agreed exist in order to avoid [xyz] consequences and realise [xyz] benefits, what can you do differently this week/day/month to begin addressing these needs?*

- What could you start/stop doing that might give you a different result?

- What impediments could you remove that might allow you to do more of what you're really good at?

- How could you think about this situation differently?

- What skills do you need to develop to better equip you to handle this situation?

Now, of course, when any of these types of question are asked, the coachee may not know what a solution is and could answer 'I've got no idea'. That is where the coach/leader might suggest any number of developmental options to help the coachee. Examples could be:

- Suggesting they get some feedback and/or ideas from other people
- Giving them something to read (e.g. article) or watch (e.g. a video)
- Suggesting a development program (e.g. training or formal coaching).

Of course, another option is for the coach/leader to actually suggest a solution. In a quantum environment, where time is of the essence, my advice is if the coach/leader has a suggested solution and has explored the ideas from the coachee first, then it is totally fine to give that suggestion. However, rather than expecting the coachee to run off and execute this suggestion, it is vital that the coach/leader return to a questioning approach to ensure the coachee understands the suggested solution and has the opportunity to expand on it.

Once a solution has been agreed upon, it is a great idea to conclude the discussion with statements such as:

- I'd like you to spend some more time planning the specific details of your action plan and then summarise this in writing so that we can review it
- I think we should revisit this to review progress and plan the next steps on [xyz] date, or every [xyz] weeks/days/months.

Phase 6 — Benefits

Once the coachee has begun the process of implementing the solutions that were agreed in phase 5, it is vitally important in a coaching approach to ensure we are monitoring for progress and testing to see if the intended benefits of the solutions are coming to fruition. Just because we have started implementing new approaches, behaviours, or strategies, the coaching is not finished.

Typically, suggested solutions rarely work perfectly straight away. Every individual, team and organisation is different, and their contexts are different and constantly changing. As such, solutions will need to be fine-tuned to suit these differing circumstances. The coach/leader needs to stay engaged with the coachee to help them refine their approach, solve problems that arise, and develop and practise new skills associated with the new approach.

Examples questions for this phase would be:

Now that you have begun implementing the agreed action plan

- What seems to be working well?
- What isn't working as well as expected? What problems have you discovered?
- How can we refine the approach?
- When can you try this refined approach?

Just as in earlier phases of this discovery methodology, the 'ask first, then suggest' approach works well for all of these questions if the coach/leader also has feedback to provide.

The critical thing is to keep the coaching going until the potential consequences that were identified have been avoided, the upsides that were identified have been realised, and the new approach is embedded as business as usual for the coachee.

Utilising diagnostic tools to assess capability

When it comes to discovering the capabilities and development needs of any entity, the old maxim 'if you can't measure it, you can't manage it' is very relevant. Without good diagnostic information, how do leaders know just what they should be focusing on when taking a coaching approach with any individual, team or organisation?

While the 'discovery methodology' I have just outlined is an incredibly powerful coaching tool, it will only ever uncover and air the views of two parties, the coachee (when they are asked the suggested questions), and the coach/leader (when they suggest things at each phase of the process). They are both very valid and useful perspectives to understand, but they are only two perspectives and may not give a complete picture.

What about all of the other stakeholders involved in working with the coachee? They will each have their own perspectives on the capabilities and development needs of the coachee. Their perspectives will have been developed from a far more diverse set of experiences and contexts than those of the coach/leader and the coachee. Getting input from these stakeholders will provide a far more complete and accurate picture of the coachee's capabilities and development needs.

There are hundreds of diagnostic tools available for use with individuals, teams and organisations. In a quantum environment, it is my opinion that tools that are simple, fast and effective should be used. A quantum leader does not want to engage in diagnostic processes that will take months to produce any useful information. The key criteria in selecting a diagnostic tool for a quantum environment is its ability to identify capabilities and strengths that the coachee may already possess, but which have yet to be effectively applied or utilised within their work environment (i.e. their capability potential).

I have already described the ECOS model in chapter 2. In my experience, this tool is a very fast and simple way to effectively obtain a high-level understanding of any individual's operating style, and then by extension, a broad understanding of their likely strengths/ preferences, and the consequences of them overplaying these strengths/preferences. I highly recommend that leaders take the time to make their own assessment of the operating styles of any individual they lead. This is an excellent starting point in identifying 'quick wins' in increasing capability.

However, if we truly want to understand how to unlock capability in individuals, we need a far more specific understanding of their unique strengths than can be provided by any kind of generic personality profile. In my 20 years of experience as an executive coach, I have not found a better strengths-based diagnostic tool than CliftonStrengths, which is owned and distributed by the Gallup organisation.

CliftonStrengths

The CliftonStrengths assessment tool was built on the back of a 40-year research project into human strengths led by Donald Clifton, and launched originally in 2001. It was subsequently updated and significantly extended in 2007 and has since been used by millions of people worldwide. The research identified and categorised 34 different strengths that are typically used by people in organisational settings. The CliftonStrengths assessment tool identifies an individual's top five strengths, with the option to produce a ranked listing of all 34 strengths. Personally, I believe the top five is all a quantum leader really needs to know in order to be able to identify useful capability potential in any individual.

The thing that makes this diagnostic tool different from many others is that as well as a generic description of each of their top five strengths, every individual receives a personalised 'insights report' which provides unique descriptions of each strength as it applies to them. In my opinion, this personal report is absolute gold to a quantum leader.

To give you an example, according to the CliftonStrengths assessment tool, my top five strengths are Strategic®, Positivity®, Woo® (Winning others over), Communication®, and Arranger®. Now, you will read those words and you will naturally attribute certain characteristics to them based on your own experiences. For example, if someone asks you to describe someone who is strategic, you will have certain characteristics that immediately jump to mind. They might be things like big picture, visionary, considered, insightful, etc. I could add many high-level generic words that could all legitimately be associated with the concept of being strategic. Of course, if I asked five different people to describe what strategic means, I would most likely get five very different descriptions. That is because there are many possible aspects to being strategic and everyone will have experienced them differently.

The beauty of the personalised insights report is that it gives me the specifics of my Strategic® strength, i.e. what is it that makes Strategic® a strength for me, as opposed to anyone else? In my case, Strategic® is a strength because of my ability to sort through clutter to find clarity, my ability to see patterns and connections, my ability to consider and develop alternatives, my ability to evaluate potential obstacles, my ability to make decisions and take action, and my ability to learn from mistakes. These descriptions resonate extremely strongly with me and provide a much greater level of granularity to understanding my strengths. The tool provides me with this same level of granularity for each of my top five strengths, as it does for everyone who uses the tool.

There are many extremely powerful ways in which my colleagues and I at Executive Central have been able to help our clients over the years by using this diagnostic tool. But one that I feel is particularly relevant to the concept of achieving a quantum leap in performance is that of getting people 'in the zone'. The 'zone' has been described as many things, but in essence it is a state of being where an individual is able to deliver peak performance with apparent ease. When 'in the zone', someone is likely to be feeling as though whatever they are doing is easy, they feel calm and at peace, they feel like things are just flowing smoothly, they even feel like things are happening in slower motion than normal, and they can anticipate things before they actually happen. 'In the zone' is often a term used by sportspeople to describe those all too rare moments where everything just seems to be 'in sync', and they achieve a level of performance at the absolute peak of (and sometimes beyond) their capabilities.

The concept of 'the zone' applies in work settings also. Many people are able to think of a time when they felt like they absolutely 'knocked it out of the park' at work. It might have been a presentation they did, a meeting with a key stakeholder, a job interview, a project they were working on, a problem they were solving, or some research they were doing. It could have been anything. If someone has ever felt like everything just seemed to go right, it felt easy, or it came together perfectly, the chances are they were 'in the zone'.

Strengths researchers have found that if someone is able to use two or more of their top five strengths at the same time in any situation or endeavour, they significantly increase the probability of being 'in the zone'. What strengths coaching is all about is helping people learn how to get themselves 'in the zone' by deliberately focusing on which of their top five strengths they can simultaneously bring to certain situations. I have seen it hundreds of times. When someone is able to do that, their performance can quite literally seem to take a quantum leap!

Having a knowledge of an individual's top five strengths and the unique personal insights behind each of them presents a powerful opportunity for any quantum leader. I guarantee that there will be many elements of people's strengths that leaders had no idea about before using this diagnostic tool. I also guarantee that there are many things that leaders could have these people doing, which they are not currently doing, to take greater advantage of their strengths. This alone represents a potentially significant way you can increase the capability factor for that individual in the quantum equation. Extend this to a broader number of people, and leaders can start to have a truly significant impact on the capability factor in the quantum equation for teams and entire organisations.

Just one last thing about the CliftonStrengths tool. It is extremely fast to deploy and extremely affordable. The cost of an individual CliftonStrengths assessment is only AUD $33 (about US $20). It only takes an individual about 20 minutes to complete, the strengths reports are generated immediately, there is no need for a formal debrief (though having a coach who knows how to get the most out of the tool is strongly suggested), and everything can be done online. It certainly fits my criteria of being simple, fast and effective — all characteristics that are required in a quantum environment.

360-degree leadership capability assessment tool

While the CliftonStrengths assessment is a brilliant tool for identifying capabilities/strengths that a person may have but which are not yet being utilised, it is also important to be able to identify the capabilities that are being displayed by an individual, and where they may have capability gaps. A 360-degree feedback tool can be a very effective way to do this.

As most readers will know, a 360-degree feedback tool is an instrument that enables people who work with and around an individual to provide feedback about that individual; 360 degrees means we are interested in feedback from every direction: self, superiors, peers, direct reports, customers, suppliers, and other stakeholders.

It is very important that leaders (and organisational development professionals) are aware that there are different types of 360-degree feedback tools, and it is important to use the right type for the right situation. At a high level, there are basically three main types of 360-degree instruments: capability-based, behaviour-based, and profile-based.

Capability-based instruments seek feedback about the individual's current, demonstrated level of performance against a pre-determined set of desired capabilities. Many organisations have developed capability profiles for key roles within their business e.g. CEO, executives, functional leaders, team leaders, etc. A capability-based 360-degree instrument simply asks respondents a set of questions associated with each desired capability. As an example, at Executive Central we have developed our own capability-based tool, which we call LCAT (leadership capability assessment tool) based around the capabilities identified in the I–We–You leadership framework, which I discussed in chapter 2.

Behaviour-based instruments seek feedback about how an individual behaves in their current environment. The important thing to realise about such tools is that the environment in which an individual is operating has a huge impact on how they behave, and hence the results that such an instrument will produce. If you change the environment, you will often change the behaviour, and changes will be apparent in the diagnostic results. These tools do not give a behavioural profile of a person (i.e. 'You always behave like this!'). This is a common mistake made by both organisations using such tools and 'professionals' debriefing them. They are very powerful tools, however, and can help an individual understand the way they are perceived by others and to identify behaviours that might serve them better in the current environment.

Profile-based instruments seek feedback about the type or style of the individual. Based on the feedback provided, an individual will be categorised into a type or style according to whatever profiling model the tool is based on. There are a number of popular profiling instruments that have options for 360-degree feedback to be gathered. We have developed our own based on the ECOS model that I outlined in chapter 2.

Each of these types of instruments has its place and, properly applied and debriefed, can add great value for an individual. In the context of quantum environments, where we are looking for speed and efficiency as well as quality feedback, my preference is for capability-based tools, such as our LCAT and LCAT Snapshot tools. From such tools, a quantum leader can get a very clear picture of an individual's current capability. It is easy to determine where they are already strong (which might be able to be better utilised) and where they have development needs (which are skill gaps that will need longer-term development).

Obviously, getting feedback from a diagnostic tool is only the front end of the increasing capability process. Once specific development needs have been identified for an individual, or for multiple individuals in a team or organisation, it is a quantum leader's role to then provide coaching which will help identify solutions and strategies to address those needs. I suggest that phases 5 and 6 of the Happy–Sad–Happy methodology discussed earlier will work extremely well, once the results of any 360-degree diagnostic tool have been provided.

In summary, using a coaching approach, supported by the discovery and/or diagnostic methods I have described, it is a quantum leader's objective to find at least one way to increase the capability factor of the quantum equation for an individual, team or entire organisation. I am not saying that quantum leaders have to address every development need that an individual, team or organisation has in the short term. They just need to find one reasonably significant way of creating an improvement in capability and contributing to the capability factor of the quantum equation.

As the quantum equation suggests, it is when an improvement or increase in capability is combined with a simultaneous increase in the trust and energy factors that a leader can excite a quantum leap in performance. The rest of this chapter explores how to achieve this.

Increasing individual capability

Once a quantum leader has determined the capability potential that any individual has by utilising one or more of the approaches outlined previously, it is critical to develop action plans to unlock that potential. Phases 5 and 6 of the Happy–Sad–Happy model outlined above are all about the development of solutions or actions to address the development needs that an individual has, and hence begin to unlock their capability potential. There is, however, more to unlocking capability potential than just coming up with a solution or an action plan.

Whenever someone tries something new, there is a very high likelihood that it is not going to work perfectly the first time. The old analogy of learning to ride a bike comes to mind. Falling off the bike a number of times is all part of the learning process. Also, the specific environment or context in which an individual is operating may require a refinement of any solution or action plan to make it suitable for that situation. In short, in any action planning process with an individual, it is vital that leaders do not assume that the job is done once an initial solution or action plan has been identified.

In quantum environments leaders need to speed up the process of learning and refining approaches to enable a more rapid unlocking of capability potential. My advice is that quantum leaders need to plan for the fact that solutions will not work perfectly, and will need refinement, and they should set these expectations with individuals up front. They then need to build in a process of refinement that can be executed rapidly.

In executive coaching, we use a process that we call the Reflect, Plan, Act cycle. In this cycle, we are initially reflecting on a need or problem that needs addressing with the coachee. We then jointly plan an action or solution. The coachee then executes the action or solution. We then come back together and reflect on how that plan worked (e.g. What worked well? What didn't work so well? What would you definitely do again? What would you change?). We then plan a refined approach and the coachee executes the refined approach, and so on. The cycle continues until we focus on something that actually works for that individual in that specific context.

This approach is totally appropriate for a quantum environment, it just needs to be executed more quickly than it might otherwise be in a more normal environment. Rather than waiting until the next one-on-one catch up with an individual (which could be weeks away) to review how things went, quantum leaders should be making the iterations of this cycle happen within days. Obviously, individuals need to have time to go away and execute the planned actions, but leaders need to ensure these actions are given high priority in a quantum environment, rather than leaving it to the individual to get around to it when they can.

In my experience, it is amazing how quickly individuals can improve their capabilities and performance when they are prepared to try new approaches as a matter of priority, learn from these attempts, refine their approaches, and try again, and then repeat this cycle as quickly as possible. In quantum environments, leaders need to play the role of a coach (sometimes educating, sometimes encouraging, sometimes pushing, sometimes supporting, sometimes just listening) to ensure this actually happens, and other distractions do not stand in the way of this release of capability potential.

Increasing capability in teams

Obviously, every team is made up of individuals. So, increasing the capability of an individual using any of the methods we have discussed earlier can also have a very positive impact on the teams that individual belongs to. But as the old saying goes, 'A champion team will always beat a team of champions!' So, increasing the capability of a team as a distinct entity is a critical skill of quantum leaders.

In 2012, my colleagues and I at Executive Central completed a detailed literature review and environmental scan on the topic of organisational team effectiveness. We knew that there were hundreds of different team effectiveness methodologies and thousands of books written on the subject, which had the potential to make it highly confusing for busy organisational leaders when they were trying to work out how to lead their teams effectively and set them up for success. We wanted to identify the most commonly recurring themes across as many of these methods as we could review, with the intention of developing a simplified process for developing superior team performance.

The outcome of our research was the development of what we now call our Superior Team Performance Coaching (STPC) suite of programs and intellectual property. At the core of the STPC suite are what we identified as the five core drivers of superior team performance:

1. Diversity of operating styles and strengths
2. Group dynamics conducive to positive team culture
3. High quality individual relationships between team members
4. Highly effective and efficient team processes and methodologies
5. A focus on continual innovation and improvement.

Each of these topics is huge in its own right and I could fill an entire book by exploring any one of them in detail, but I would like to focus on one fairly radical idea that I believe could enhance all of these drivers if it were to be implemented effectively. Without doubt, this approach can provide quantum leaders with the 'quick wins' that can produce an immediate, significant improvement — a quantum leap — in the capability of teams. Moreover, I believe implementing this new approach to how teams are structured and changing the way team members are expected to behave will also provide a huge improvement in the levels of trust and energy that are present in any team. This idea hits the quantum jackpot because it will contribute to all elements of the quantum equation for teams simultaneously. I am going to introduce the term 'quantum team structure' to describe this initiative, which I truly believe can be a game changer.

Introducing the quantum team structure

Almost every team development or team building activity I participated

in during my corporate career involved some form of profiling tool that helped the team to identify the different personality types or operating styles of the individual members of that team. There are scores of different profiling tools that get used for this type of profiling and most of them, in my experience, are excellent.

However, what tends to happen in these activities is that all of the attention is put on the profiling exercise and very little attention is put on what I call the 'So what?' I have had people come up to me 10 years after they have done some kind of profiling exercise as part of a team workshop or a leadership program and proudly tell me their 'type': 'Oh yes, I remember this profiling stuff. 'I'm an explorer/promoter'; 'I'm a C on the DISC model'; 'I'm a peacock'; 'I'm a driver'; 'My top strengths are Maximiser®, Futuristic®, etc.' And on and on it goes. It seems that we all love to label ourselves regardless of what tool we use.

At an individual level, stopping at the profiling and forgetting to focus on the 'So what?' is a very common problem. As we have already discussed in chapter 2, emotional intelligence is all about achieving superior results and relationships with and through others. Self-awareness, which profiling can assist with, is only the first step. Awareness of others, which profiling can also assist with when a team goes through the exercise together (but which is often difficult to do with many tools in everyday life), is the next step. But the real driver of emotional intelligence is someone's ability to use their awareness of self and others to decide on actions and behaviours that are going to deliver better results. We called this 'flexing' to achieve better results.

The exact same reasoning applies at a team level. Inevitably, if you determine the individual style profiles and identify the unique strengths of the members of a team, you are going to find that there is diversity in that team. It is easy to fall into the trap, as I have seen many teams do, of just sitting back and congratulating themselves on being such a diverse group of people. But just having diversity in a team's makeup does not mean that it is helping the team. Put simply, there are two possibilities. A team's diversity can either work for it or it can very much work against it. How a team executes the 'So what?' as a result of understanding the diversity within it will determine which of these possibilities become a reality.

Let me describe my proposed quantum team structure and explain how it can increase a team's capabilities by utilising the diversity of styles and strengths in that team.

Structure teams on function *and* capabilities/strengths

Going to the effort of profiling the styles and strengths of their team members is well worth it as long as leaders then put that knowledge into action. Another way of saying it is that unless the effort of profiling a team results in the leader doing something significantly different, what is the point of profiling them?

The core concept of strengths-based leadership and positive psychology as espoused by people like Donald Clifton, Daniel Goleman and Martin Seligman is that individuals will achieve far greater outcomes and feel a much greater sense of wellbeing if they are utilising their strengths. If we extend that thinking from individuals to teams, teams will achieve superior results and have a much greater sense of trust and energy if team members are utilising their strengths.

I believe quantum leaders should fundamentally change the way they organise their teams. I believe that quantum teams (teams operating in quantum environments) need to be organised and managed by both function *and* by capabilities/strengths.

In every team I have come across, the primary criterion for structuring the team is the functional responsibilities of each team member e.g. you look after sales, you look after finance, you look after operations, you look after people and culture, you look after marketing, etc. It does not matter what level the team is, functional responsibility is currently the primary determinant of who the members of the team are and how the team is structured.

My advice — and it might seem radical, but quantum environments are radical — is that in quantum teams, members should formally be given two core responsibilities. The first responsibility is still the oversight of their function (with some important enhancements to how they do this), but the second (and equally important) responsibility is that they must make available and deploy their own strengths/capabilities across the entire team (i.e. in all other functions) and actively take advantage of the strengths/capabilities of their teammates to help in their own functions.

Let me use my time as a member of the executive leadership team (ELT) of Compaq Computer in the late 1990s as an example. If our ELT had been structured as a quantum team, instead of just being the functional head of the Consumer Division, I would have had two core responsibilities. One would have been leading the consumer function, the other would have been to make my CliftonStrengths of Strategic®, Positivity®, Woo®, Communicator® and Arranger® readily available to every other function of the business. Very importantly, part of my responsibility as the leader of the consumer function would have been to be fully aware of and appropriately access and deploy the core strengths of the other members of the ELT for use within the Consumer Division.

Now, I am not just talking about some occasional favour that one team member might do for another. I am suggesting that it would have been one of my key performance indicators to ensure that every other function within the business had access to my strengths and, equally, that I would have been accessing the strengths of every other ELT team member.

As a consequence of this, I would have been accountable for the performance of not only my own function but all of the other functions as well. Indeed, if any function was to struggle in any way, our CEO would not just have been focusing on what the functional leader would need to do to fix the situation, he would also have been holding the rest of the team accountable to find better ways to help fix the situation by utilising each of our strengths.

Let's think about how this might work in practise, using the example of the CFO of Compaq Computer Australia back in the 1990s. Obviously, one of his core responsibilities was the oversight of the finance function of the business. Under the system I am suggesting, part of the CFO's functional responsibility would have been to be aware of and access the identified strengths of other members of the ELT to assist him in running the finance function. So, if the finance function had a need to communicate effectively (be that internally or externally), one option for the CFO would have been to leverage my CliftonStrengths of Communication® and Woo® to help achieve that more successfully. Or if the finance team needed some help in strategic problem solving or system innovation, the CFO might have asked for my help using my Strategic® and Arranger® strengths. Very importantly, it would have been my responsibility to ensure I made it a priority to make these strengths and capabilities available to the finance team.

The really powerful thing would have been that the CFO could also have called on the unique strengths of every other member of the ELT to meet their needs as well. With that arsenal of strengths and capabilities to call on, I struggle to think of a problem that could not have been solved or a situation that could not have been addressed.

On the flipside, as a member of the ELT, the CFO would have been required to make his unique strengths available to me (and everyone else in the team) to help me run my function. So, I might have required help with an element of research, financial strategy, problem identification, governance, risk mitigation, knowledge of processes, or whatever else. In any of these cases, the CFO's strengths would have been of immense value to me and would have required me to spend less time trying to become an expert in things that I was not naturally strong at.

While it might sound like I am suggesting that under this system, people do not need to learn new things or focus on their areas of weakness to continue to improve as executives and leaders, the truth is, every team member gets the opportunity to learn from the strengths of every other team member. The difference under this approach is that every team member is exposed to those strengths on a regular basis in the normal course of the team conducting business. In most teams currently, exposure to the strengths of other team members is at best a very occasional thing.

I can hear you asking, how on earth will a busy executive have time to be helping out these other functions when they have already got so much to do in their own function? This is a really important question. Clearly, some things need to change about the way executives currently operate. So how can leaders find the time to work in a quantum team the way I am suggesting?

Efficiencies generated by the quantum team structure

To find the time to make their own strengths and capabilities readily available to all other functions, members of quantum teams need to spend less time 'down in the weeds' of their own functions. Unsurprisingly, this is already an issue that comes up regularly in coaching assignments with executives. So, apart from implementing some of the delegation strategies that we have already discussed in chapter 2, each member of a quantum team also needs to be setting up their own team to run the same way, fully leveraging the strengths of each team member across the team.

If this cascading of the quantum team structure is applied throughout the organisation and everyone is working towards and sharing their strengths, quantum team members will be able to confidently and successfully delegate to their teams many of the tasks that currently take up their own personal time. More time will then be available for their second core responsibility — making available and deploying their own strengths across the other functions of the organisation.

Another major efficiency created by the quantum team structure is to reduce the number of issues and subjects that need to be addressed by the full team. One of the concepts that I believe needs to change in quantum environments is the assumption that teams are not working as a team unless everyone in that team is all together as a team. In my opinion, having everyone together at the same time in the same place is often a recipe for dysfunction and inefficiency, and leaders need to realise that their team can still function effectively if it is physically apart.

Let me clarify what I mean. I am not saying that teams should never come together and be in the same place at the same time. Obviously, there are important reasons why teams need to come together on a reasonably regular basis in some form of team meeting. I believe, though, that most organisational teams try to do far too many things when they are all together at the same time in the same place. (I include video-conference meetings, which are extremely relevant in the new world of Covid-19 restrictions, as being together at the same time in the same place.)

One of the core elements of the diversity of styles and strengths within a team is that different people like to go about things in different ways. The way people think, strategise, solve problems, make decisions, communicate, analyse, deal with pressure, etc. are all extremely different. Yet, if we are trying to do any of these things when the team is all together at the one time and place, we are forcing at least a significant proportion of team members to work in a compromised way. More specifically, we are likely to be forcing people to perform in one of the following ways: the way the leader likes to perform, or the way the more dominant members of the team like to perform. Clearly, that approach is not going to get the best out of everyone in the team.

My advice is that quantum leaders need to be far better at giving people the opportunity to leverage their strengths and preferred styles by employing any or all of the following approaches:

1. Let team members work on things on their own or in smaller sub-teams and then share their results or input with the leader

and/or broader team. This increases the likelihood that people will work to their strengths when they work away from the main group

2. Ensure people are given the opportunity to take a question on notice and go away and think about their response rather than having to respond on the spot. Many senior teams tend to require their members to respond to issues on the spot without having time to analyse things and/or consider things carefully. This disadvantages many people who are less expressive or less comfortable with talking 'off the cuff'

3. Be very clear about what mode the team is in whenever it is together. There can often be a mix of strategic, tactical, operational and individual-specific issues that get thrown into the same team meeting. People get confused and frustrated when they are not sure how the team is meant to be handling each issue and how, correspondingly, they are individually expected to behave.

Implementing the quantum team structure might sound like a massive change to the way teams currently work, and in a lot of ways it is! It is my belief that the biggest change needs to be how we currently think about organisational teams, how we set them up and how we measure and manage them. Currently, we set up silos from the very start by structuring teams by function only. The quantum team structure is all about playing to people's strengths and, as such, I have found that team members can very quickly adapt to this way of working, and they love it! When the unbelievable improvements in results, relationships, culture and energy all begin to flow, it becomes hard to imagine working any other way.

Key success factor — coach every team member to continually improve their emotional intelligence

For the quantum team structure to work, it relies very heavily on the emotional intelligence of team members, and particularly, how they use this emotional intelligence with each other. Without it, there is no way that the structure could ever work.

The ability of quantum leaders to coach their team members to continually improve their individual emotional intelligence and use it with their teammates is mission critical. There is one thing I can assure leaders of, which is that no-one ever crosses the finishing line in the race to emotional intelligence. When dealing with other people, we can never have them completely worked out. There will always be a new scenario, a new context, a new problem, a new pressure, etc. that can challenge the way an individual deals with any other individual.

It is very important that quantum leaders keep challenging their team members to keep trying and refining the way they deal with their teammates. It is very easy for people to get comfortable with their teammates, assuming they have got it all worked out and that 'all is good'. It can therefore be a rude shock when the proverbial stuff hits the fan and suddenly those same people are not so easy to deal with.

Considering the changed behaviours that are required from every team member to make the quantum team structure ways of working successful, it is clear that these would require team members to be able to interact with each other in ways that require significantly more finesse than traditional team approaches require.

We have touched on some basic coaching skills already in this chapter, but in the context of the quantum team structure, the most important thing for quantum leaders to do is to make time for this type of coaching with team members. Again, the question needs to be asked — where will quantum leaders find that time? It has got to come from freeing themselves up from tasks and activities that should be undertaken by their team members. It has also got to come from de-prioritising the time-wasting habits and activities that can distract from higher order leadership activities — like coaching people!

Increasing capability of organisations

There are potentially a million topics that could be discussed under this heading. Obviously, organisations are made up of individuals and teams, so any of the increasing capability suggestions I have already made, if implemented successfully, are likely to have an impact on the capability of any organisation.

Given that I am focusing on the capabilities of organisations operating in quantum environments, I would like to focus on four capabilities that I believe are absolutely critical in such an environment. They are capabilities that can produce a quantum leap in the performance of organisations and increase the level of 'future-proofing' those organisations possess.

The case for building innovation capability

In rapidly changing environments, an organisation's ability to innovate is, in my opinion, the biggest determinant of how the organisation will emerge from each change it encounters. What I mean by this is that each time an organisation is impacted by some kind of change in its operating environment, it will either come out of that change in a stronger position or a weaker position. The current Covid-19 period is a tremendous example of this. Some organisations have innovated incredibly quickly and will emerge in the 'new normal' in a stronger position than ever. Others have struggled to innovate and are craving the 'good old days' of pre-Covid, hoping to return to those conditions as soon as possible. These organisations may find that there will never be a bounce back to pre-Covid conditions and they may emerge significantly weaker.

In my experience, an organisation will very rarely emerge from change in the same position. The degree to which the organisation is able to innovate in response to that change will determine whether it ends up stronger or weaker, and to what degree. If leaders think about this stronger/weaker scale, they should acknowledge that in many of the case studies that are often cited around the subject of innovation, we only ever hear about organisations that found themselves at the extremes of this scale.

For example, I am sure many people have heard the stories of Nokia, Kodak, Blockbuster Video, PanAm and others. As a result of their failure to innovate (or even recognise the changes that were affecting them) these organisations ended up at the extreme end of the 'weaker' scale, i.e. they either went out of business or were massively downsized and/or restructured. Equally, many tales of the organisations who achieved market dominance as a result of their superior innovation capability have been told; names like Apple, Tesla, Google and Uber are often bandied around.

Of course, there are many very important lessons that can be learned by looking at these 'extreme' cases. Clearly, a failure of organisations to recognise (and take seriously) changes and disruptions that are happening in their environments, and then failing to innovate accordingly to respond to those changes and disruptions is a recipe for ultimate disaster. Equally, having highly innovative cultures is clearly a major competitive advantage for those who have come out on top.

However, the danger in looking at the extremes of any bell-shaped curve is that it is sometimes very hard to relate to them and imagine how our own organisations could ever duplicate such extreme outcomes, be they good or bad. What I believe to be more instructive is to acknowledge that most of the time, organisations will tend to come out either slightly stronger or slightly weaker as a result of changes they encounter. Often these slight changes can be hard even to notice, but they are absolutely there!

In my experience, with changes happening all around, it is quite common to find that organisations will just charge ahead doing what they normally do without changing at all. In change theory, this is called 'denial', where people ignore the change and hope it will not affect them. It is quite possible that these organisations might get lucky and come out slightly stronger as a result of the change. But more commonly, they will come out of the change slightly weaker. I have no research to back up this statement, but my experience and gut feeling says that across all of the changes an organisation encounters, if they do not innovate at all and just keep operating in a business-as-usual fashion, about 80 per cent of the time they will emerge slightly weaker from change and 20 per cent of the time they will emerge slightly stronger. Obviously, as these organisations encounter more and more changes, the odds really start working against them and they will eventually be coming out significantly weaker as a result of the ever-changing environment.

It is a very interesting exercise for leaders to sit down with their teams and reflect on the changes that have impacted their organisations in the past 12 to 24 months. Just remembering them can be hard, but it is usually quite an eye opener to realise just how much change has been encountered. The next step is for leaders and their teams to honestly ask themselves whether their organisation came out of each change in a stronger or weaker position. Elements that might be considered are competitive position, market share, ability to influence, quality of relationships, brand reputation. Next, ask the question, 'Did we deliberately innovate in response to a change?' (Note: changes that they were forced to make, e.g. by a regulator or by law, do not count as innovations.) What leaders need to reflect on is whether their organisations actually took the time to reflect on the changes and the issues they presented, understood these deeply, creatively developed response options, and deliberately selected the options they wanted to implement.

Sadly, I believe the usual outcome of this exercise, if it is done honestly, is that the vast majority of organisations identify a huge number of changes that they have encountered, but can only identify deliberate innovations for a very small number of these changes, if there are any at all. If my 80:20 assumption applies, this means that many organisations find themselves on a slow but steady spiral into weaker and weaker positions as a result of their changing environments. To avoid this slow and steady decline, quantum leaders need to focus on building the core capabilities of innovation across their entire organisations.

The four capabilities of innovation

In late 2019, I was very fortunate to be introduced by my Executive Central colleague, Jane Counsel, to Professor Michael Anderson from the University of Sydney, Australia. Jane lectures on diversity and inclusion as part of the University of Sydney's MBA program, and Michael, who is a professor in the School of Education, also lectures in the MBA program. Jane thought that there might be an opportunity for Michael and me to collaborate on the subject of innovation, which is such a huge emerging issue for so many of our clients.

It turned out that Michael and his colleague Miranda Jefferson had just published a book titled *Transforming organizations — engaging the 4Cs for powerful organizational learning and change.* It also turned out that this book was the first that I had found that really talked about the core capabilities that are required within organisations if they want to successfully innovate. In my experience, organisations talk a lot about the need for innovation, but do not really know how to develop the capability of the organisation and its people to actually innovate. This book really brings that problem into specific relief and provides practical and pragmatic solutions.

Needless to say, I love the book and would highly recommend it as a worthwhile read in its entirety. Michael Anderson and Miranda Jefferson conducted extensive research in the education and business sectors to identify these core capabilities, and then used their expertise as educators to develop methodologies that can help organisations embed them to enable effective responses to emerging challenges, threats and opportunities.

So, what are these core capabilities of innovation? The four capabilities (the '4Cs') that Michael and Miranda identified as absolutely vital in organisations needing to be more innovative are **creativity, collaboration, critical reflection,** and **communication.** Michael and Miranda contend that each of these capabilities can in fact be learned and ingrained into an organisation's culture. They also identify the very important inter-relatedness between the four. In other words, you really need all four of these capabilities to be in place if your organisation is ever to innovate effectively.

I will not attempt to cover each of these topics in anything like the detail that Michael and Miranda have in their book. Instead, I highly recommend that you read it yourself! For the purposes of this book, let me extract a couple of the key ideas that I feel are potential 'quick wins' for quantum leaders.

Building creativity capability

In their book, Michael and Miranda introduce a 'coherence maker' called the 'creativity cascade'. This is a metaphorical cascade with four stages (or pools) that support creative processes. It suggests a process where each level of understanding feeds into the next, just like water cascading under the influence of gravity from one pool to the next.

I really like this concept and think it suggests a process that any organisation operating in a quantum environment needs to develop as a key cultural practice. In fact, I think the concept of the creativity cascade is so powerful that I am going to describe the other '3Cs' in terms of how they actually enable it.

The first stage of the creativity cascade — **noticing**

Essentially, this is all about taking the time and energy not only to perceive an issue, problem, change, opportunity, situation, etc. but to achieve a deep and connected perspective about it. In my experience, in the modern workplace there are so many things competing for the attention of individuals and teams that they will tend to be perceived at a very shallow level. There is a tendency to think that there is not enough time to get through everything, so we just deal with them based on our first impressions.

At an individual level, just think about how most people deal with their email inbox. If someone comes back to their desk, checks their emails, and finds that in the last couple of hours they have received 50 new emails, what do they do? Most people tend to scan through them very quickly, trying to identify any that might be important. They then delete as many as possible and probably just answer as many of the easy ones as they can to reduce the list as quickly as possible.

At a team level, particularly a leadership team level, just think about how many issues often find their way onto the agenda of team meetings. There will be issues that the leader wants to address, there will be issues that team members want to address, there will be issues that get put on the agenda by people outside the team (e.g. presentations to the leadership team), issues in the marketplace, major project updates, problems that need solving, etc. Having such a busy agenda of items to get through makes it very hard to spend any quality time properly perceiving them, let alone dealing with them!

I also suggest that, whether at an individual or team level, in modern organisational life there is a 'rush to action'. People seem to feel that unless they are getting to an action, they are failing. Of course, they do need to get to a point where they eventually decide on actions, but in the context of 'noticing', this 'rush to action' results in many people failing to take the necessary time to properly perceive and understand the issues they are addressing.

As an example, an internet search on the topics 'problem solving' or 'decision making' identifies hundreds of suggested methodologies on how to do these things successfully. In virtually every one of these, the first step is always 'define the problem'. Having worked with scores of executive teams over the years to help them get better at problem solving and decision making, it never ceases to amaze me that when we try and apply a methodology to a real-life issue, the 'define the problem' step shows just how many different perceptions of the core problem exist among the members of the team. Unless we take the time to consider all of these different perceptions, we run the risk of 'rushing to action' and solving something that is not the real problem, or making a decision about the wrong thing.

In the context of the creativity cascade, the key message I take from the 'noticing' stage is that it should not be rushed. It is vital that individuals and teams slow down and take the time to engage their powers of perception to notice things (issues, problems, needs, opportunities, behaviours, processes, functions, patterns, relationships, habits, etc.) at a far greater level of detail than they might normally do. This includes tapping into the diversity of the people all around them to understand how they might perceive these things differently.

How the other 3Cs contribute to **'noticing'**

As I have already mentioned, in their book, Michael and Miranda spend quite a bit of time showing how all the 4Cs are closely interconnected. Without doubt, that is certainly the case when it comes to the 'noticing' phase of the creativity cascade. I believe **critical reflection** capability is essentially a deeper form of noticing.

Put very simply, critical reflection could be defined as a reasoning process to make meaning of an experience. So, in the context of 'noticing', it means taking the time to reflect on an experience and deeply analysing what happened so that lessons can be learned and ultimately applied to future experiences. To be truly valuable, this reflection process needs to reflect on more than just 'what' questions, such as 'what was done?' and 'what happened?' It also needs to look at 'how?', 'why?', 'who?', and 'when?' questions to critically assess the experience. This means the reflection needs to consider things like politics, power, relationships, behaviour, and cultural norms, and those doing the reflection need to be able to do this with full 'agency', i.e. having the appropriate power and ability to speak up and act.

As an example, let me share with you an experience I recently had with a corporate client of mine. The organisation had asked me to conduct some leadership development workshops for middle managers with a particular emphasis on a number of topics that had been identified as real 'issues' within the organisation. One of those issues was the inability of these managers to properly prioritise tasks and manage their time.

If I was just to stop at the 'what is happening?' question, I would have only heard about the projects that were running overtime, the poor quality of work that was being submitted, the failure to do important things like performance management of staff, and so on. It was clear that the senior leaders had only asked the 'what is happening?' question.

When I started to explore some of the 'how' and 'why' type questions with the managers themselves, it became very apparent that the issue was not only about the capability of the managers. There were issues concerning the use of power within the organisation and particularly from the CEO's office. There were issues about a strong cultural bias to say yes to everyone. There was historical evidence of people who had been punished for questioning directives from above. The list went on and on.

You can see that if I had just bowled into the workshops and facilitated sessions only about prioritisation and time management methods, I would have only been scratching the surface of the true needs of those managers. I would have essentially been solving the wrong problem. Thankfully, I did ask the 'how' and 'why' questions and the workshops became far more about strategies to appropriately influence upwards, respectfully pushing back or saying no, balancing the power dynamics in any situation, and so on. It became a totally different workshop to the one I was originally asked to provide.

I firmly believe that most organisations do not practise quality critical reflection and therefore spend an awfully large amount of time solving the wrong problems or making decisions about the wrong things. I think the main reason organisations do not practise critical reflection is the time it takes to do it properly, and the vulnerability it must necessarily create. We have already discussed the time issue and how there is a 'rush to action' culture in many organisations but allow me to touch briefly on the issue of vulnerability.

To get the full value from quality critical reflection, everyone involved needs to be prepared to be vulnerable. Those who were involved in the experience that is the subject of the reflective practice need to be prepared to have their actions, behaviours, and practices critically reviewed. That does not mean it is all going to be negative, but when someone asks why someone did something in a particular way, or behaved in a particular way, or suggests that there might have been alternatives, it is very hard for most people not to become defensive in some way. Equally, those who are conducting the review need to be prepared to be vulnerable and ask what might be uncomfortable questions, or potentially 'dumb' questions, or challenge an expert or a superior.

In my experience, the best way to get people comfortable with being vulnerable is to first show your own vulnerability as the leader. I have come across plenty of leaders who were very good at making other people feel vulnerable, but they did not like it one bit when the shoe was on the other foot! Vulnerability is a true 'lead by example' opportunity. If leaders are prepared to have their own actions, practices, behaviours, etc. subjected to critical reflection, particularly by subordinates, and they make this experience a constructive one for all involved, then the impact of that can spread like wildfire throughout the organisation. This also gives leaders the right to expect the same preparedness to be vulnerable from other leaders and staff throughout the organisation.

I encourage leaders to read some of the more detailed processes that Michael and Miranda suggest in their book around critical reflection. In summary, the quick win that leaders can achieve in building organisational capability around critical reflection is to make quality time for it to occur and make themselves (or something they have been intimately involved in) the subject of it.

Without doubt, the other 2Cs, communication and collaboration, have a very strong contribution to the quality of the 'noticing' phase of the creativity cascade. However, I feel their biggest contributions come later in the cascade, so for now, let's move on to the next phase.

The second phase of the creativity cascade: 'Ask why, really why?'

Only when this deeper level of noticing and greater level of curiosity has been engaged, are we ready to move to the next stage of the creativity cascade — **'Ask why, really why?'** This next phase is all about taking the deeper observation of 'what is' that is gained from the 'noticing' phase, and building an understanding of 'why it is'.

I am confident many leaders will have come across any number of enquiry methods in their careers which encourage the user to dig deeper to get beneath the surface of an issue or situation. The 'Ask why 5 times' is one such method, where the enquirer asks 'Why?' at least five times to get the responder to provide a much deeper level of explanation about a topic. Let me try and give you an example of how this approach works.

Initial question: What is your favourite thing about your job?

A: I really like interacting with customers.

Q2:   Why do you like interacting with customers?

A: I enjoy dealing with a wide variety of people.

Q3: Why is dealing with a variety of people enjoyable?

A: It means that I don't get bored dealing with the same people all the time.

Q4: Why does dealing with the same people all of the time make you bored?

A: I hate predictability and it becomes predictable when I'm dealing with the same people all of the time.

Q5: Why do you hate predictability?

A: If I know what is going to happen, I don't feel any excitement or thrill in what I'm doing.

Q6: So, what you're really saying is that a really important thing about any work you're doing is that it is exciting and thrilling. Would that be a fair statement?

You can see from this kind of example that it is really important not to act just on the first answer you are given because you would be acting on the wrong thing. If I was to act on the first answer in this example, I would be looking for any opportunity for this person to work with customers as a way of making their work enjoyable. If I was to give this person a job working with customers who were very stable and predictable, I would be getting it completely wrong. What this person really enjoys is excitement and thrills, and there might be many other ways I could provide that other than just dealing with customers.

Another technique we use a lot in executive coaching is called 'funnelling'. I have already described this technique in chapter 2 as a way to improve the ability to flex when dealing with other people. However, it is also an incredibly powerful way to gain a much deeper understanding of an issue. As a reminder, the idea of funnelling is similar to the 'Ask why 5 times' method, but instead of asking 'Why?' all the time, we ask specific follow-up questions about something in the other person's previous answer. Using the same example above, applying a 'funnelling' approach might sound like this:

Initial question: What is your favourite thing about your job?

A: I really like interacting with customers.

Q2: What is it that you like most about dealing with customers?

A: I find it exciting dealing with a wide variety of people.

Q3: What is exciting about it?

A: I like having to be on my toes every time I go into a meeting with a new person. You never know what you're going to find. They might be really friendly, they might be unfriendly, they might be aggressive, they might be passive. I love having to work that out and then react accordingly.

Q4: So how do you 'work them out'?

A: I try and get them talking about something about themselves or their business. Most people are happiest when they are talking about themselves, so I just use this to get them talking. I can usually find out a lot about a person from this.

Q5: So once you've found out about them, what do you do next?

A: I try and adapt my approach to them to make them feel more comfortable. Some people like to get to the point, some people like the social chat, some like a lot of facts and detail. I just try out some strategies to see if that makes them comfortable.

So, while this approach also elicits a deeper level of understanding, it can provide a bit more flexibility to dig into the topics the enquirer is particularly interested in.

Both of the methods I have provided as examples are ways that anyone can do a good job of the 'Ask why' part of this stage. However, what I really like about this method is the 'Really why' part of the enquiry. This moves beyond just getting a deeper understanding of a situation as it appears or is described and tries to explore the background reasons why something is the way it is.

In *Transforming organizations*, Michael and Miranda use the example of the question, 'Why do we struggle to create diverse workplaces?' The initial responses to this question could be things like, 'People struggle to get on with each other', or 'People are intolerant of difference'. But when we ask 'Really why?' we push beyond the first superficial response and search for deeper answers. In this case, we could well uncover issues such as racism, stereotyped views of who can do what, biases (both conscious and unconscious), social norms, and organisational culture, to name just a few.

The 'Really why?' element is critical to the creativity process as it drives a depth of understanding of the real issues that need to be addressed and focuses the creative process on developing solutions that will be truly meaningful. Solving the wrong problem, or a superficial perception of the real problem, ultimately means that creativity is useless and certainly fails to contribute to any true innovation.

How the other 3Cs contribute to **'Ask why, really why?'**

I am sure you have already noticed that the 'Ask why, really why?' phase is in itself a form of critical reflection. It tries to uncover why things happened, not just what happened. But I believe this phase of the creativity cascade particularly relies on **communication** skills to be truly valuable.

If you consider either of the enquiry methods I suggested earlier ('Ask why 5 times', and funnelling), I suggest that the communication skills of the enquirer are the key determinant of the quality of the enquiry. In particular, the enquirer's listening skills are critical. The ability to ask a question and then suspend your own thoughts, opinions, experiences, and judgement to be truly present and listen intently to the answers provided, and then being able to form the next question based on what was heard, is, in my opinion, sadly something that is not done well in our organisations, or in society more broadly.

There is a two-pronged benefit deriving from leaders practising quality communication with an emphasis on quality listening. First, the quality of the information that is gathered is far better when the quality of listening is better. Obviously, that means the actions, decisions, or learnings that are generated from that information are likely also to be far higher quality than would otherwise be the case, and ultimately the business outcomes generated are equally improved.

Second, the positive emotional response a leader is likely to get from the person being questioned when they feel they have been truly listened to can be significant. These positive emotions feed directly into the level of trust, comfort and engagement that person is likely to feel towards the leader and the organisation, and also the level of energy and wellbeing they feel. As we have already discussed, trust and energy are the other key factors of the quantum equation, so through the power of listening, leaders can truly knock it out of the park!

The third phase of the creativity cascade is 'playing with possibilities'

Once we understand 'Really why?' we are ready to move to the next stage of the creativity cascade, **playing with possibilities**. This phase is all about coming up with options for how the situation or issue that was noticed and then deeply understood in the previous two phases might be addressed.

One thing that I really like about this phase, as it is described in *Transforming organizations*, is that the authors have deliberately used the word 'playing' to emphasise the importance of creating an environment where people can get away from their normal 'serious' business persona and explore/try out things that might seem crazy on the surface. When children play, they use their imaginations, they pretend, they role-play, they do not mind being silly or having a good laugh. Unfortunately, as Michael and Miranda point out in their book, we tend to lose the ability to do a lot of these things as adults, and that really impairs the creative process.

There are far too many methods designed to get people to use their imaginations for me to provide an extensive coverage here. However, I do believe that many of them revolve around getting people out of their normal 'mode' of operating and making it okay for them to ask or suggest anything they like.

One absolutely brilliant example of doing both of these things is a process that I first came across when I read a book called *Nuts! Southwest Airlines' crazy recipe for business and personal success*. This book, by the way, is probably the best book I have read about creating powerful organisational cultures, so I highly recommend it to you.

The method I am referring to is called 'Walk a mile in my shoes', and it involves getting people from different parts of the organisation to 'ghost' or follow each other around and then ask questions about why things are done the way they are. So, as an example, when Southwest Airlines was trying to develop a system that would enable it to turn around any plane in ten minutes (i.e. the time from when the plane parks at the gate to when it backs away on its next flight), it used this method as a way to find massive efficiencies. Baggage handlers followed pilots around for a day or two and asked a bunch of questions that challenged the pilots' processes; engineers followed the cabin attendants; refuelling crews followed the flight operations teams.

Having people who have no technical or functional understanding of what a particular group does asking questions and making suggestions can often result in established conventions being challenged and more creative ways of achieving things being considered. Creating a climate where there is no such thing as a 'dumb question' or a 'dumb suggestion' is also critical. It takes a lot of discipline and resilience for any function in an organisation to be prepared to be questioned and avoid the desire to respond with 'That's just the way it has to be', or 'It's technical, you wouldn't understand'. If there is not a simple and logical answer to a question, which can be explained to a person who is not an expert, then often it is worth really questioning why something is done.

Just to finish the story about Southwest Airlines, they did successfully achieve the '10-minute turn' which enabled them to cover the routes they needed to with fewer aircraft and significantly reduced expenses. The solutions they developed involved many radical departures from what was considered normal and best practice for airlines at the time (late 1960s), and paved the way for many lower cost airlines to make air travel a realistic option for many more people than had previously been the case.

Another very common way to 'play with possibilities' is to look at the way organisations in different industries operate and explore whether their approaches could help to address needs in your own organisation. We have done this many times over the years at Executive Central. One great example was when we were first setting up the organisation and we wanted to come up with a consultant fee structure that was fair to both the consultant and to the company in terms of risk and reward. At the time, my sister was in the real estate industry and had been telling me about a tiered commission structure that her organisation used to compensate its real estate agents. After quite a bit of investigation and tweaking to our specific needs, we ended up developing a structure of consultant fees that was fundamentally similar to this real estate model. That model served us very well for our first decade of operations.

The other thing I would like to emphasise about the 'playing with possibilities' phase is the importance of playing with possibilit**ies** — plural. This phase is not just about coming up with one good idea. True creativity often involves rejecting numerous possibilities or ideas before finally settling on a way forward. We cannot do this without multiple possibilities to consider.

In practice, it is very difficult to resist the urge of jumping into action planning when you have come up with what you think is a good idea. Starting again and developing other good ideas and other possibilities can be extremely frustrating, particularly to people who have a strongly results-oriented style! In my experience, and I have done this personally on numerous occasions, it is very common for people to get excited about one idea and then want to get on with making it work. Holding back and properly playing with other possibilities is not a skill I have seen a lot of people demonstrate. Yet, done well, it will definitely improve the probability that whatever you eventually do choose to do will be successful.

How the other 3Cs contribute to 'playing with possibilities'

My very strong view is that the 'playing with possibilities' phase is where the ability of individuals and teams within an organisation to **collaborate** becomes a mission critical capability. **Collaboration** can be simply defined as two or more people working together to complete a task or achieve a goal. In the context of the creativity cascade, the goal those people are working together on is the generation of possible ways to solve a problem, meet a need, or take advantage of an opportunity.

Again, I would like to emphasise just how important the earlier phases of the creativity cascade are in the context of collaboration. Getting clarity around what problem they are trying to solve is what focuses the collaborators' minds and ensures they are all pulling in the same direction. I have seen many well-intentioned collaborations fail when the involved parties were not clear on what they were actually collaborating on.

As mentioned earlier, the ability to generate multiple possibilities is critical in this phase. Good collaboration practices will help with this. In *Transforming organizations*, Michael and Miranda outline a structured, four-phase collaboration process which I really like. They talk about offering, yielding, challenging and advancing. I will leave you to read the detail on each of these in their book, but I was particularly drawn to the concepts of offering and yielding.

Offering and yielding is an iterative process whereby collaborating parties will make offerings (of ideas, suggestions, information, experiences, knowledge, etc.) and other parties will yield to these offerings by considering them, adding to them, enhancing them, exploring them, reshaping them, and so on. And then, once an offering has been taken as far as it can go, new offerings might be made by other collaborators and the yielding process follows again. This process allows multiple possibilities to be considered and then a selection made for deeper challenge and advancement.

Clearly, quality **communication** skills are required to make all phases of the collaboration process effective. Each collaborator needs to be able to enunciate their offerings clearly and listen effectively to the contributions of others during the yielding process. When possibilities are selected for deeper challenge, the ability of collaborators to challenge clearly and to listen in order to understand and ask clarifying questions, without defensive behaviours appearing, is a key success factor.

The final phase of the creativity cascade is 'selecting and evaluating'

When we do have a number of creative possibilities to consider, the final stage of the creativity cascade, **selecting and evaluating**, is where it is vitally important to switch out of the 'creative' mode and into the 'discernment' mode. This phase is where we need to come back to reality and evaluate the possibilities that have been developed against what we know to be possible, the reality of our organisations, the financial possibilities, our experience, our markets, etc. It requires discipline, business acumen, and rigour to ensure we are making a selection based on logic and not purely emotion.

In my experience, in this phase it is a good idea to have people who are not the owner of an idea to evaluate it. It is human nature to become emotionally attached to ideas we have been part of developing and disregard any evidence that might question that idea. This is known as 'confirmation bias' and it is all around us in our world today. In short, it can be described as only paying attention to evidence that supports your position or opinion and disregarding evidence that does not support it. As an example, I think both sides of the climate change debate have demonstrated unbelievable confirmation bias. Political parties in most countries also suffer massively from confirmation bias. Sadly, many organisations suffer just as badly when it comes to their own views of the markets in which they operate.

To ensure our creative processes actually evolve into true innovation, a robust evaluation and selection phase is absolutely vital. We have only truly innovated when we have applied a creative idea and it has actually solved a problem or met a need. Carefully evaluating our options and then selecting the option(s) that pass muster is the only way we can possibly make this a reality.

How the other 3Cs contribute to **'selecting and evaluating'**

Again, elements of every one of the other 3Cs are required if the selecting and evaluating phase is going to be robust and effective. Critical reflection capabilities will ensure the evaluation process has depth, communications capabilities will assist when engaging in debate and decision-making as part of the selection process, and collaboration capabilities ensure that there is a shared ownership and responsibility across each possibility being considered, thus avoiding any sense of 'winners and losers' in the selection process.

Evaluating organisational capabilities

As I have already mentioned, I decided to focus on innovation as a critical capability for organisations operating in quantum environments because it is the one thing, in its many forms, that can shield organisations from any negative effects of radical and sudden changes in their operating environments. I have suggested that the 4Cs — creativity, critical reflection, collaboration and communication — as outlined by Michael Anderson and Miranda Jefferson in *Transforming organizations*, are organisational capabilities that leaders can focus on increasing, potentially to achieve 'quick wins'.

However, as I have already spoken about in the previous sections on 'Increasing individual capability' and 'Increasing team capability', before leaders try to implement development solutions, it is important that they are able to get a snapshot of the organisation's current level of capability. This is true also of the 4C capabilities.

In partnership with 4C Organizations, which is Michael Anderson's consulting practice, Executive Central has developed an 'organisational innovation effectiveness' (OIE) assessment tool that measures an organisation's current levels of capability against the 4Cs. In fact, the tool measures nine sub-capabilities in detail, down to individual team level within the organisation, and provides an overall OIE score as measured against other organisations in similar industries.

Armed with this kind of quantitative data, leaders can identify the specific innovation capabilities that need development in each part of their organisations, and appropriate development solutions can then be explored.

CHAPTER 4

Increasing trust in individuals, teams and organisations

Trust is a very interesting word and an equally interesting concept. It is a word that is used extensively in the values, mission statements and codes of ethics of many organisations. Trust is something that just about every organisation wants from its customers and stakeholders. It is something that just about every person wants to be given from anyone with whom they interact. It is also something that just about every book written about leadership refers to, often from many different perspectives. In short, trust is quite a complex subject.

In the context of quantum leadership, when I talk about trust the focus needs to be on how leaders can increase the level of trust that individuals, teams and organisations feel as quickly as possible. Regardless of which entity we are talking about, even a small increase in trust, when combined with corresponding increases in capability and energy, can result in a quantum leap in performance.

My intention in this part of the book is to identify methods that I have experienced and learned about that can help quantum leaders quickly and significantly increase the level of trust that is felt by whichever entity they are focusing on. It should be acknowledged that long-term trust is something that cannot be rushed. My belief is that there is a difference between trust that is given and trust that is earned. For example, I might give someone trust because I believe in their capabilities. But the trust that they earn from me by using those capabilities to deliver a successful outcome is a far stronger and deeper trust.

To help leaders understand the subject of trust and its many different aspects, I really like the way Stephen M Covey covers the subject in his book *The speed of trust*. Covey describes trust as being something that is not just 'touchy-feely' and 'nice to have', but something that is a hard-nosed business asset that can deliver quantifiable economic value. When trust is high, speed of execution (in just about every aspect of organisational life) goes up and costs go down. When trust is low, speed of execution goes down and costs go up. Covey describes a high trust environment as equating to a dividend, and a low trust environment as equating to a tax!

Covey describes the ability to build trust as the most important competency that any leader can have. While he acknowledges that there are many other competencies a leader must have to be successful, his view is that every one of these is made easier and more achievable if the leader is able to build trust first. I strongly agree with his view from a competency perspective. It is hard to think of anything that a leader needs to do in the modern organisational environment that is not better achieved if that leader is trusted and there is a high trust environment in that organisation.

In a quantum environment, the relevance of the impact of trust only becomes greater. We have already discussed the premium that must be placed on innovation in a quantum environment. Every one of the 4Cs that drive innovation — creativity, collaboration, critical reflection, communication — will be achieved far more successfully if they are happening in an environment of trust. My view is that without trust, rather than creativity, collaboration, critical reflection and communication, leaders will get tentative and conservative suggestions, forced interactions, avoidance of criticism, and lots of talking and very little listening!

Very interestingly, in the context of the quantum equation, Covey also specifically describes a relationship between trust and energy. In short, he states that in high trust environments both energy and joy increase, but in low trust environments both energy and joy decrease. Covey states that this energy can present in many different forms, such as the level of engagement, passion, creativity, innovation, and discretionary effort displayed by people. The joy he describes can be the happiness of individuals, the fun in teams, and the levels of satisfaction measured across an entire organisation, each of which also correlate very strongly to the levels of energy in an organisation. So, increasing trust is also likely to play a part in increasing energy at the same time. This is great news from a quantum equation perspective!

One aspect of Covey's take on trust which I really like is that he has identified that trust exists, and can be lacking, at different levels. I believe all of these levels are relevant to quantum leadership. Covey calls these levels 'the five waves of trust'. I think it is worth exploring each of these waves as they provide leaders with a useful hierarchy of trust and help to identify the current level of trust felt by an individual, team or organisation, and where the leader's focus may need to be directed in order to increase the trust factor of the quantum equation.

Self-trust

Self-trust is the trust that you feel in yourself. It is derived from an individual's abilities and capacity to set and achieve goals and keep commitments. When an individual has a high sense of self-trust, they feel self-confident and self-content. This inner sense of contentment and consistency then makes it possible for an individual to be worthy of the trust of others.

In describing this wave of trust, Covey suggests that the key driver of self-trust is credibility. He proposes 'four cores of credibility': integrity, intent, capabilities, results. If an individual is to have complete self-trust, they must 'pass muster' at each of the cores of credibility. If any one of these four cores is lacking, then self-trust will be lacking. These four cores of credibility also play a huge part in how other people trust an individual (relationship trust), how people trust their organisations (organisational trust), and how the customers trust an organisation (market trust). If an individual, team or entire organisation is falling short in any one of these four cores of credibility, trust will be diminished.

In short, the four cores of credibility can be determined for any individual by having them answer the following questions:

Integrity — Do you do what you say? Do you act in ways that align with your personal beliefs and values? Do you say what you really think? Are you the same in private and in public? Do you keep confidences?

Intent — Do you have an open and clear agenda? Are you seeking a win-win outcome? Do you care about the wellbeing of others? Do you act in the best interests of others? Does your behaviour show that you truly care about what you say you care about?

Capabilities — How relevant are your capabilities to your role and/ or the task at hand? What are your natural gifts and strengths? What are your attitudes and world views? What skills have you become exceedingly proficient at? What knowledge have you gained? What is your operating style, your way of getting things done?

Results — What is your track record? What evidence is there to show what you have produced? What tangible results are you generating day-in and day-out? How are you going about getting those results?

I use these four cores of credibility extensively in my coaching because it helps to clarify what someone means when they use the word 'trust' in some kind of 'headline' statement. Examples of such headline statements are, 'You just can't trust him!', 'We've got trust issues in our team!', 'I don't trust myself in situations like that!', and 'Don't you trust me?' In all of these examples, it is really useful to dig beneath the headline statement using the four cores of credibility to try to identify where the issue really lies.

As an example, I was once asked the 'Don't you trust me?' question by an employee when I was conducting a performance discussion with her. She held a very senior sales role in our business, and she had fallen way behind her sales target. We had had a number of smaller discussions over an extended period of time to try and help her to rectify the situation. She had suggested many reasons why things were not working, which were all about other people being at fault. She would say things like 'I know what I'm doing', and 'I've seen all of this before and things will turn around'. But it had reached the point where if things did not improve markedly, we would be forced to look at moving her on from that position.

When I raised the prospect of her employment being at risk, she asked me 'Don't you trust me?' I was able to use four cores of credibility in my answer to her. I answered her honestly and said that I had complete faith in her integrity, that I believed her intent was always positive and constructive, that she had sales capability and experience that were all extremely relevant, but that I did not have trust in her ability to deliver the results we needed because all of the evidence at hand showed that she had not delivered in the past and was unlikely to in the future. Specifically, she had achieved less than 60 per cent of her annual sales target and had very little in the sales pipeline that would indicate an uplift in the sales performance any time soon.

When she considered this response, she actually accepted that my position was 'fair enough' and accepted that the current situation was not delivering a 'win-win' for both parties. We agreed that we needed to put some short-term turn around action plans in place. As it turned out, about a month later she decided to hand in her resignation based on the fact that she was not confident that she would be able to turn her results around. Even though the outcome was not what either of us wanted, we managed it in a way that was respectful to both parties which meant that she left on good terms.

Relationship trust

To explain relationship trust, I will use the analogy that Covey uses in his book *The speed of trust*. He states that relationship trust essentially boils down to a matter of how you establish and subsequently increase the virtual 'trust accounts' that you have with other people. The key to relationship trust is all about behaviour — acting consistently at all times and in all situations. Covey identifies 13 different behaviours that 'high trust leaders' consistently exhibit. In summary, these behaviours are:

1. Talk straight — always be honest and up front about what you are thinking

2. Show respect — respect the dignity and feelings of everyone you come into contact with

3. Be transparent — be completely open about the facts and tell the truth in verifiable ways

4. Right wrongs — when you end up being wrong, work very hard at making things right

5. Show loyalty — always give credit where it is due and acknowledge others' contributions

6. Deliver results — establish a track record of getting the right things done

7. Get better — keep upping your game by increasing your personal capabilities

8. Confront reality — address the tough issues and acknowledge what is unsaid

9. State expectations — always discuss your expectations so they are clearly defined

10. Be accountable — accept that the buck stops with you and take personal responsibility

11. Listen first — listen in order to understand deeply before you respond

12. Meet commitments — say what you are going to do and then follow through and deliver

13. Extend trust — demonstrate your ability to extend 'smart trust' to others

I like the 'trust account' analogy because, like bank accounts, it is possible to make deposits and withdrawals from the 'trust account' you hold with any other individual. Making deposits is fairly easy to understand. Anything you do to increase the trust that someone else feels towards you is essentially a deposit and increases the balance of that account. This is just the same as a person depositing cash into a bank account to increase the balance.

The concept of withdrawals is where 'trust accounts' and bank accounts differ slightly. With bank accounts, cash needs to be withdrawn from the account, thus reducing the balance, before that cash can be used for a purpose (e.g. to buy something or to invest in something). With 'trust accounts' the great news is that the trust that has been built up in an account does not have to be withdrawn before it can be used. As an example, if I have built up a high level of relationship trust with a teammate, I might use that trust to ask that teammate to do me a favour. If that teammate subsequently does that favour for me, it does not mean that they now trust me less (i.e. my 'trust account' has not been reduced).

Of course, it is possible to reduce your 'trust account' with other people by doing anything that reduces the level of trust felt by that person. We could certainly define this as a 'withdrawal' and, obviously, this is the type of withdrawal to be avoided. Sadly, individuals can and do make these types of withdrawals, often without even realising!

This is where I think the 13 behaviours are particularly useful. Clearly, if an individual demonstrates these behaviours consistently, trust will increase in that relationship, thus increasing the 'trust account'. On the other side of the ledger, it might be easy to think that to decrease the 'trust account', individuals would need to do the opposite of each behaviour. Certainly, behaving this way would indeed diminish trust, and diminish it very quickly. Any leader who demonstrated the opposite of these 13 behaviours would not be successful in any sustained way and more often than not, would not be a leader for very long.

However, I do not think behaving the in opposite manner is the biggest problem. My suggestion is that simply failing to display these behaviours (as opposed to doing the opposite of them) also diminishes trust. Further, failing to behave consistently leads to major trust depletion. There is no place for 'fair weather friends' when it comes to building trust. In other words, a leader cannot just display the desired behaviours when it is easy or convenient to do so. The leader must also display the desired behaviours when it is not easy to do so. That is when people really know that they can trust the leader's behaviour.

In the work my colleagues and I at Executive Central do with teams, one of the drivers of superior team performance that we focus on is the importance of high quality, interpersonal relationships within the team. During the exploration of this topic, we provide a hierarchy of relationships to help team members consider what type of relationship they have with each other member of the team. While we apply it to the relationship between team members in that context, it can equally be a way to assess the status of the relationship any individual has with another person. I think it is a very practical example of how the different elements of trust, as outlined in the four cores of credibility and 13 trust building behaviours, can exist in all types of relationships, but to have the highest quality of relationship, you need all of them acting together.

In this hierarchy, we identify four different types of relationships which can be summarised as follows:

Types of stakeholder engagement

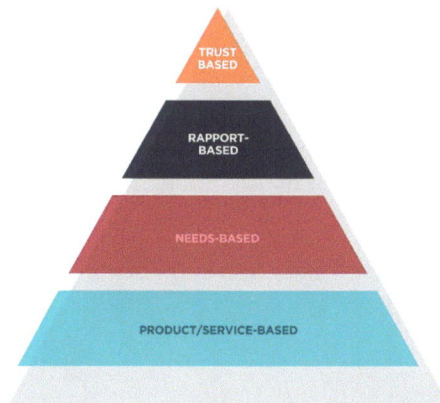

TRUST BASED

RAPPORT-BASED

NEEDS-BASED

PRODUCT/SERVICE-BASED

Product or service-based relationships

These are transactional relationships where the basis of the relationship is purely the product or service each person offers, e.g. 'I need a lawyer. You're a lawyer, so you'll do.' If either party has a need for that product or service, they will interact with the other party. If neither has a need for the other's product or service, they are not even thinking about each other.

This is not a bad relationship, but it is the lowest quality in the hierarchy because anybody else who offers the same product or service might have the same quality of relationship with the person in need of that product or service. There is a level of trust that exists in this type of relationship but it is purely based on the capabilities that are associated with each person's role or function.

Needs-based relationships

These are also transactional relationships, but they are based on the fact that one or both of the parties are able to meet a specific need for the other and have proven that in the past, e.g. 'I've bought a new property and need some conveyancing. Last time, you were the lawyer who did my conveyancing, so I'll use you again.' Again, the parties will only tend to think of each other when the specific need exists. If the need does not exist, they do not think of each other.

This is a higher quality relationship than a product or service-based relationship because one or both of the parties have actually earned a greater degree of credibility because they have not only proven their capabilities, they also proven their ability to deliver results.

Rapport-based relationships

People in this type of relationship have some kind of rapport between them that transcends any specific transaction. In other words, they have something in common, be that a shared experience, a shared interest, or a shared relationship. This means that they would more than likely have something to talk about at any time they might come across each other and, therefore, do not rely on a 'transaction' to bring them together.

I believe this is a critical transition point in the relationship hierarchy because this is the point at which people can make a conscious decision to spend time with and find out more about another person. This is something that can be achieved by putting in some effort.

This is a much higher quality relationship than the previous two types because to have built rapport, the parties are likely to have spent time together in some form and have found something interesting about the other person, more than just what they do. Either or both of the parties are also likely to have gained some insight into the integrity of the other party and the way that person behaves.

Trust-based relationships

This is the highest quality of relationship, but the hardest to achieve. My definition of a true trust-based relationship is one where both parties have absolute confidence that the other party has their best interests at heart and would represent these best interests at any time in any situation. The reason each party has such confidence is that it has been earned, i.e. it has already happened in the past.

The reason this is the hardest type of relationship to achieve is that you cannot force it to happen. No matter how much effort you put into trying to elevate a relationship to this status, to truly have proof that someone will represent your best interests, even if you are not physically present, requires a real situation where this has actually happened. It may take a very long time for such a situation to occur, so true trust-based relationships may take a long time to develop.

The reason this is the highest quality of relationship is that all of the four cores of credibility are proven, particularly that of intent. By representing the best interests of the other party, even when that other party was not present, each person has proven that their intent is truly to achieve a win-win outcome.

Organisational trust

The essence of Covey's concept of organisational trust is the degree to which an organisation's systems, structures, policies, processes and frameworks (I call these the operational ecosystem) suggest that people are trusted or not trusted. He states that people work best when they are placed in a high trust environment rather than one where everything is locked down tight.

Obviously, organisations need to have quality operational ecosystems if they are going to be able to operate with good governance and high quality in a reliable, repeatable and predictable manner. I am certainly not suggesting in any way that organisations should not have such operational ecosystems developed and effectively implemented. Like Covey in *The speed of trust*, I am suggesting that when systems and processes are set up in a way that suggests they are more about catching people out for doing the wrong thing, or that people are incompetent, as opposed to making things reliable, repeatable and predictable, then there is a major organisational trust problem.

Organisations that have a low trust environment tend to become very inefficient and bureaucratic because no-one is trusted to know their job, or do their job, and there are high levels of redundancy and duplication of effort. The quantity of rules and policies and processes tends to increase continually in what I see as a naïve attempt by the leaders of those organisations to completely remove the risk of there ever being a mistake. Unsurprisingly, such organisations have very low staff morale and engagement, high turnover of staff and customers, poor customer service, and ultimately disappointing results.

I have already talked at length in chapter 3 about the importance of innovation in modern organisations, particularly in quantum environments. How on earth can people ever innovate if the operational ecosystem of their organisation is so strict, inflexible, and risk averse that nothing new will ever be tolerated, including new ideas? If there is absolutely no tolerance within an organisation of mistakes and everything is set up to avoid them, then by definition, there is no tolerance either for innovation and the inevitable mistakes that are part of the innovation process.

An interesting analogy to consider is that of the human body's auto-immune system. The auto-immune system is vital to the survival of the human body, playing a mission critical role in regulating the environment within the body and resisting foreign bodies like germs and viruses. When the body is healthy and working perfectly, the auto-immune system maintains that status quo. But sometimes, when the body develops a major problem, for example a severe organ problem, in order to survive the body requires a transplant. Medical science has made it possible for a patient to receive a donated organ in order to survive. However, the biggest threat to the viability of that new organ is the body's own auto-immune system which sees it as a foreign body and attempts to reject it. So, even though that new organ is the one thing that the body needs to survive, the auto-immune system still sees it as a threat and tries to reject it.

The operational ecosystem of an organisation is its auto-immune system. When things are going well and the organisation is healthy and successful, this operational ecosystem is a tremendous asset in maintaining the status quo. But if the organisation becomes unhealthy and requires a transplant, such as an important innovation to what it does or how it does things, there can be a huge risk that the operational ecosystem attempts to reject it in order to maintain the status quo. Even though the innovation might be the very thing that can help the organisation survive, the operational ecosystem sees it as a threat and tries to reject it.

So, just as doctors and scientists have had to develop anti-rejection drugs in the medical world to enable successful organ transplants, so too do leaders need to develop anti-rejection habits and behaviours that enable successful innovations. To do this, leaders need to interrogate the operational ecosystems of their organisations regularly to ensure they have not crossed over from the 'light side' of efficiency, reliability, repeatability, predictability, to the 'dark side' of fear, distrust, suspicion, and restriction.

Before we leave the organisational trust wave, I would like to add another element that I believe plays a huge role in the level of trust felt throughout an organisation. That is the degree to which the behaviour of leaders is consistent with the stated values of the organisation. Put simply, if leaders walk the talk of the stated organisational values, people will trust them and the organisation. If they do not, as can often be the case, people will trust neither them nor the organisation. It only takes one leader to openly and consistently behave in a way that is not consistent with the organisation's stated values for organisational trust to begin diminishing rapidly. It is very easy for all leaders to become 'tarred with the same brush' when this kind of behaviour is tolerated.

Over the years, both in my own corporate career and in my consulting and coaching practice, I have seen organisations spend huge amounts of time and money developing values statements. Often, there is an intense focus on the 'word-smithing' of these value statements to get them looking and sounding just right. Unfortunately, often nowhere near as much time is spent assessing whether those values are actually practised within the organisation. Sadly, there is often a huge gulf between the stated values and the practised values.

When you think about most organisations' value statements, somewhere in there will be something about topics like 'People', 'Customers', 'Innovation', 'Integrity/Respect' and 'Courage'. While no-one would ever expect a leader to behave perfectly in alignment with such statements 100 per cent of the time and in every possible scenario, they most certainly would not expect a leader ever to behave in a manner that is completely at odds with these statements. Unfortunately, in some organisations, leaders do not only behave at odds with the values, they are seen to be rewarded for it!

To my way of thinking, people have a fairly simple mental model when it comes to values. If leaders say something is important and then behave consistently in line with what they have said, then they can be trusted. If they do not, they cannot! Given leaders are seen as the principal representatives of the organisation, then if the leaders cannot be trusted, the organisation cannot be trusted, and if the organisation cannot be trusted, then people will simply engage in what I call 'safer pursuits', i.e. they will never take risks or do anything more than the basic requirements of their jobs. This is hardly a recipe for organisational success in a quantum environment!

In summary, to ensure high levels of organisational trust, apart from considering the four cores of credibility (self-trust) and 13 trust-based behaviours (relationship trust) that we have already discussed, every person in a leadership position throughout the organisation needs to interrogate the operational ecosystem over which they are presiding and consider how their own behaviour aligns with the stated values of the organisation (organisational trust).

Market trust

The fourth wave of trust as described in *The speed of trust* is market trust. This is really all about how the brand of an organisation is viewed in the market. In other words, its reputation.

Leaders really need to consider that an organisation tends to be viewed as a single entity by the market. The level of trust that entity has in the market is driven by exactly the same four cores of credibility and 13 behaviours of relationship trust that determine the degree to which an individual is trusted. The only difference is that it is the cumulative effect of the behaviours of everyone in the organisation and every interaction those individuals have with the market that determines the organisation's level of market trust.

To determine what an organisation's level of market trust is, leaders need to consider questions like:

Does our brand have integrity?

Do we have a reputation for being honest?

Do we face things head on?

Do we provide stakeholders and customers with evidence that shows our stated values are actually our true values?

Does our brand demonstrate good intent?

Do we aim to deliver a win-win result for our customers and stakeholders?

Do we focus on our long-term impact or short-term results?

Do we make it clear why we are doing things?

Is our brand associated with positive connotations?

Do people associate our brand with excellence and quality?

Do people perceive our brand as being innovative?

Do people see our brand as a leader or a follower?

Is our brand associated with delivering positive results?

Do we deliver what we promise to our customers and stakeholders?

Is our brand consistent in its performance?

Does our brand's track record provide the evidence that we can be trusted?

Once these questions have been considered, if the answers are not what a leader would want them to be, then a good place to start determining what needs to be done is to ask this question: *Do our people demonstrate the 13 behaviours consistently to the market?*

If they do not, then the first thing I suggest needs to happen is to focus on anyone who holds a leadership or management position in the organisation and investigate the extent to which the 13 behaviours are being demonstrated by them. If leaders want the people of their organisations to demonstrate any kind of behaviour, that behaviour must first be demonstrated by those same leaders.

To demonstrate why I am so adamant about this, I can tell you that over the last 20 years that I have been delivering leadership development programs (supported by coaching), there have been scores of examples of frontline managers asking me the question, 'If what you're telling us is the way leaders should be behaving, why aren't our senior leaders behaving this way?'

I strongly advise my clients that before they start any kind of leadership development program, they should take a serious look at the behaviours and habits of their senior leaders and ensure they are consistent with what is going to be covered in the program. If they are not, then the senior leaders should actually participate in the program themselves to show that they are committed to this way of working. This is all about building trust by actually walking the talk of the behaviours and values that are being espoused by the organisation. If a development program is being sponsored by the organisation, even if it is being delivered by an external provider, then the organisation is seen as espousing what is being covered in the program.

To close on the subject of market trust, when I think about this topic I am always reminded of another book I read many years ago called *Moments of truth* by Jan Carlson, the former president and CEO of Swiss Air. The core premise of the book is that every single interaction anyone in an organisation has with any stakeholder of any kind (he particularly focuses on customers), is a moment of truth. In that moment of truth, the stakeholder gets to see what the organisation is truly made of, what its true values are, and what it will really be like to deal with this organisation over the longer term. Reputation is built through the cumulative effect of these moments of truth, so every person's behaviour should be regarded as critical.

Societal trust

The final wave of trust as described by Covey is 'societal trust', which at its heart is all about contribution to society or the greater good. Societal trust is increased when people, and the organisations of which they are a part, are seen as giving back rather than taking, and when the contribution they make is seen as building a healthier, fairer, more vibrant, safer society.

Many organisations have realised the importance of societal trust as a social and economic necessity in the modern era. Measuring and reporting a triple-bottom line which considers social and environmental contribution as well as financial contribution when considering the performance of an organisation has become more commonplace. In my experience, most senior executives realise that a balance between profit, people and the planet, is far more than just a 'nice to do', it is a 'must do'.

It is at this wave of trust that I would also like to make a very strong link to the topic of energy, which is the third factor in the quantum equation. One extremely powerful source of energy in individuals, teams and entire organisations can be their strong belief in, and alignment with, the purpose of the organisation. Put simply, if people believe in the purpose of the organisation, they will be energised to go above and beyond what is expected of them to help achieve that purpose.

When I talk about purpose here, I am not just talking about the 'word-smithed' purpose statement that sits in a frame up on the wall in head office, or that is splashed around on PowerPoint slides at company meetings. I am talking about the 'real' purpose of the organisation — what people feel and experience in their everyday work, and the impact they see their work actually having. If the real purpose is something that people believe in, then they will not only feel societal trust in themselves and their organisation, they will be hugely energised.

This concept of the 'real' purpose is both an opportunity and a threat for leaders. Sometimes, it can be hard for people to see the end result or impact of their work beyond the contribution their work makes to the financial results of the organisation, because that is what the organisation focuses on every day. What people may struggle to see is the impact their efforts are having in society or the contribution the organisation is making to the greater good.

My suggestion is that leaders need to go far beyond just reporting a triple-bottom line when discussing the performance of their organisations. They need to ensure the discussion of the societal and environmental contribution the organisation is making is shared and experienced by every person in some way.

Trust and quantum leadership

As Covey suggests in *The speed of trust*, each of the waves of trust really build from the earlier waves. If any wave of trust is missing, there is no way that later waves of trust can follow. Given its link to speed, cost, energy, and joy, I strongly align with Covey's statement that trust is the one thing that can change everything. We have already discussed how increased trust will increase energy. Increased trust will also significantly help to increase capability because, by definition, to build capability, individuals, teams and entire organisations need to feel safe to try new things, make mistakes, learn from mistakes, and try and try again. Trusting oneself, other people, and the environment within which one operates is the only way this will ever happen.

Given that the objective of a quantum leader is to increase the trust factor in the quantum equation at an individual, team or organisational level, the four cores of credibility and the 13 trust building behaviours offer a very productive starting point in this process.

Increasing individual trust

It is impossible for leaders to be able to determine how much self-trust individuals have in themselves. However, leaders can consider the role they have played in contributing to that person's self-trust by asking themselves the following questions:

- How have I demonstrated that I trust the integrity of that person?
- How clearly have I acknowledged the intent of that person?
- How have I recognised the capabilities of that person as being relevant and helpful?
- How have I acknowledged the results that person has delivered?

Another critical thing which leaders must consider with respect to the issue of self-trust is how that person would score the leaders themselves against the four cores of credibility and the 13 trust building behaviours. Leaders should ask the following questions:

- How have I displayed integrity to that person?
- How have I made my intent clear to that person?
- How have I demonstrated my capabilities as being relevant and helpful to that person?
- How have I delivered outcomes/results with respect to that person?

- How consistently have I demonstrated the 13 trust building behaviours?

It is critical that leaders answer these questions from the individual's perspective, not their own. As a check point, I suggest asking this follow-up question after each of the previous questions: What evidence does this person have to support that answer?

My experience has certainly been that individuals feel a greater level of self-trust (and self-confidence) if they trust their leader and their leader trusts them back. If this trust, in both cases, is across all four cores of credibility, as outlined in *The speed of trust*, then that trust will be very deep and powerful indeed. To achieve any kind of immediate uplift in the level of trust an individual is feeling, finding and addressing the upside available in any one of these four cores could be a very productive line of enquiry for a quantum leader.

Increasing team trust

At the team level, it is simply a matter of considering the same set of questions above, but this time from the perspective of how team members will answer them with respect to their teammates and the team leader. To produce an increase in the level of trust that a team has, I have found that any one of the four cores of credibility and 13 trust building behaviours can be fertile ground for improvement within teams. If any one of them is lacking within a team, just focusing on improving it could provide enough of an improvement in the trust factor to help generate a quantum leap in the team's performance.

Beyond this, another area to focus on is to find ways to elevate more of the relationships within a team further up the relationship hierarchy. Put simply, the more rapport-based and ultimately trust-based relationships there are in a team, the better.

In chapter 3, I proposed the quantum team structure as a way of structuring teams based on both functional responsibility and the unique strengths of each team member. As discussed in that chapter, the idea of this structure is all about breaking down functional silos in teams and unlocking the full potential of each team member across the organisation.

One additional benefit of such a structure is that it results in all team members working together a lot more often. This extra time spent working together, achieving things, solving problems, making decisions, etc. will also significantly increase the probability of team members getting to know each other, building rapport, and ultimately building trust between each other. This will have the effect of moving relationships within the team up the relationship hierarchy. This is yet another reason that leaders should consider implementing the quantum team structure that I have proposed.

Increasing organisational trust

I believe there are two very practical steps that leaders can take to create a sudden and significant increase in the level of trust that is felt by people throughout their organisations.

The first is to scan the operational ecosystem of their organisation (i.e. systems, policies, procedures, conventions, structures) and identify just one element of that system that has become more about distrusting people (the dark side) than it is about reliability, repeatability, predictability (the light side). Then, work with the people who are negatively affected by this element of the operational ecosystem to make it better.

This one act is likely to drive a significant increase in the level of trust felt throughout the organisation. Obviously, the more of these elements that a leader can identify and fix (with the help of the affected people), the greater the increase in trust. Often, just one change is all it takes to create an environment where others will feel safe to challenge the status quo of the organisational ecosystem.

The second step that leaders can take is to genuinely assess how consistent the behaviour of the organisation's leaders (at all levels) is compared to the stated values of the organisation. This assessment could be made by seeking feedback from staff, looking for evidence of desirable and undesirable behaviours, and looking at the behaviour of staff in response to the environments created by their leaders (i.e. the leaders' impact). Again, if just one behaviour that is not consistent with the stated values of the organisation can be identified and changed for the better, the levels of trust within the organisation can be increased dramatically.

CHAPTER 5

Increasing energy

Energy can be described in many ways. *The Macquarie Dictionary* provides the following entries in its definition of the word energy: 1. Capacity or habit of vigorous activity, 2. The actual exertion of power; operation; activity, 3. Power as exerted, 4. Ability to produce action or effect, 5. Vigour or forcefulness of expression. All of these definitions link the word energy very strongly to words like action, activity, exertion, power, force, vigour. In my view, these are all words that describe characteristics that any leader hopes there is an abundance of in their organisations.

To explain the concept of increasing the energy factor of the quantum equation, I think it is very important to consider the concept of energy as it is described in physics, the branch of science concerned with the nature of matter and energy in the universe. In physics, energy is described as the ability to perform work. Energy is also something that is conserved, i.e. energy cannot be created or destroyed, only transformed from one form to another.

There are two basic forms of energy, kinetic energy and potential energy. Kinetic energy is the energy of motion. If an object is moving, it is said to have kinetic energy, and the faster it is moving, the more kinetic energy it has. Potential energy is stored energy. If energy is in this form, it is not yet being applied to anything and is not yet creating action or movement.

A good example to demonstrate how these different forms of

energy work is to think of a simple rechargeable battery. When we first buy a battery, it usually comes fully charged. This means it is full of potential energy. That energy is stored in the battery, but until the battery is connected to some kind of circuit, it does not produce any kind of action or effect — it is basically a fairly useless lump of metal. When the battery is connected to a circuit, however, the potential energy (charge) is converted to kinetic energy in the form of electrical current, which is the movement of electrons throughout the circuit. This kinetic energy can then be used to produce action or effect in the device that the battery is connected to, which will usually involve some other kind of movement (kinetic energy again). This transfer of potential energy to kinetic energy will continue until the battery is depleted of its potential energy (charge). At this point, the battery needs to be recharged by connecting it to a charger where the kinetic energy of the mains electricity (current) is converted to potential energy (charge) in the battery, and the whole cycle can start again.

When I think about this process, it occurs to me that there are some very important things for leaders to consider. First, if a battery has no charge, it is a useless lump of metal. So, the process of charging and re-charging the battery is critical if the battery is ever going to be of any use. Second, even if a battery is fully charged, it remains a useless lump of metal until it is actually connected to a circuit so that charge can be converted into current which then powers the device to do whatever it is designed to do. So the process of connecting the battery to a circuit is also critical.

To understand the importance of the energy factor in the quantum equation, it is helpful to think of every person in an organisation as being just another version of a rechargeable battery. It is the energy stored within those people that can then be applied to produce an action or effect. Therefore, to ensure people do not become the human version of a 'useless lump of metal', quantum leaders need to consider the two critical elements: 1. How is each person being charged up to ensure they have got potential energy stored up and ready to use? 2. How is each person being connected to a circuit to ensure their potential energy is being converted to kinetic energy that then creates the desired action or effect?

Increasing potential energy

Unfortunately, charging or recharging a person is not as simple as plugging them into the mains power. There are many ways in which human beings build up their stores of potential energy. Some of them are physiological, e.g. we convert the energy that is stored in food into energy that is stored in our bodies through good digestion. Some of them are psychological, e.g. we are capable of increasing our potential energy through positive emotions or through relationships with others. While there are far too many ways to cover here in which humans can increase their potential energy, I will touch on some that I believe quantum leaders should consider.

It is also important to remember that there are many ways in which human beings can have their potential energy drained. The obvious one is if they use it all up by converting it to kinetic energy in the performance of work — something we would want them to spend their energy on. However, it is also possible for physiological and psychological factors to deplete potential energy levels before that energy has even been used.

An example of a physiological factor that depletes potential energy would be high stress levels which result in high levels of the chemical cortisol in the body. If this chemical is present at elevated levels in the body, that person will be constantly on a physical 'high alert', with energy (e.g. blood flow) being sent to parts of the body in readiness to react to some form of danger in the surrounding environment. An example of a psychological factor that depletes potential energy would be a person working with someone with whom they have a poor relationship, or who has a style of working that frustrates that person.

The important thing for quantum leaders to realise is that in any person's life, there will always be things that 'charge' that person and other things that 'discharge' that person. The key thing is to consider what the 'nett effect' of the energy balance is for any person. Quantum leaders need to consider whether a person is in a 'nett charged' or 'nett discharged' state. A 'nett charged' state is where the chargers in a person's life outnumber the dischargers. In this state, a person is capable of delivering work, achieving outcomes, and making things happen pretty much indefinitely, because they have got more than enough potential energy to convert into kinetic energy.

If a person is in a 'nett discharge' state, obviously there is eventually going to be a problem. If people continue to try and operate in this state for any kind of extended period, it is likely that any number of issues will begin to appear and then perpetuate if nothing is done to alter that state. These issues may take many forms but could include a decline in the quality of work output, a decline in behaviour, a decline in relationships, and a decline in both mental and physical health. Obviously, if a quantum leader fails to address this kind of discharged state, the person concerned, the teams that they are part of, and anyone in the organisation that is involved with that person, will experience any number of undesirable consequences.

Increasing kinetic energy

If a person is appropriately 'charged' and has potential energy stored, just like our rechargeable battery from the previous analogy, two important considerations for quantum leaders are whether that person is being connected to a circuit at all (i.e. is the person's potential energy being used or just lying dormant?) and, if they are connected, is it to the circuit we want them to be connected to (i.e. is the person's energy being spent on what we want it to be spent on)?

I have seen many examples of people in organisations who have incredible potential failing to apply that potential or turn it into useful action or effect. This can be caused by many factors, some of which I will discuss shortly. The impact of this, though, is that the person ends up being the human version of the 'useless lump of metal' described earlier in the battery analogy. A huge part of a leader's responsibility is to make sure people are connected to the metaphorical circuit that is the organisation's purpose, or the outcomes their work is meant to contribute to. Without feeling this connection, people will keep most of their potential energy all stored up and unused in any way.

I have also seen many examples of people in organisations who have a huge amount of potential energy which gets converted into kinetic energy by being connected to a circuit, only it is the wrong circuit. This is where people end up spending all of their energies on activities that are not helpful to the organisation. These activities could be negative office politics, gossiping, undermining other people, tasks that are not priorities, things they are concerned about but have no control or influence over, or activities that are unrelated to their work (and a million other things). These things not only deplete the energy of that person, they also deplete the energy of many other people around them.

The 4Ms model

How do quantum leaders increase both potential and kinetic energy? I would like to propose a framework which I believe provides quantum leaders with a pragmatic approach to increasing both the potential and kinetic energy of people in their organisations. This model is built around the 4Ms: motivation, morale, meaning and modelling.

Motivation

Put simply, if people are motivated, they have more energy. So how does a quantum leader ensure that people are motivated?

There have been many theories postulated over the years to try and capture the components that contribute to motivation. Maslow's hierarchy of needs, which I used in chapter 1 to identify the quantum levels at which individuals can exist, is a model that is frequently used to describe what motivates people. Abraham Maslow proposed in 1943 that an individual's motivating factors will be determined by the level at which they currently sit in the hierarchy. This kind of thinking was supported and extended by Alderfer in his ERG theory (existence needs, relatedness needs, and growth needs), and McClelland in his theory of needs (achievement needs, affiliation needs, and power needs).

For the purposes of motivating people in quantum environments, I am attracted to a model known as Herzberg's two factor theory. This model, which is also known as the motivation-hygiene theory, was developed by Frederick Herzberg in 1987. He identified that certain factors in a person's environment had the ability to increase that person's level of motivation. He called these motivating factors. He also identified that certain other factors in a person's environment did not have the ability to increase motivation, but they most certainly did have the ability to reduce it if those factors were not adequately in place. He called these hygiene factors.

The following table summarises Herzberg's theory:

Motivating factors	Hygiene factors
Achievement	Policies and procedures
Recognition	Supervision

Nature of work	Salary
Responsibility	Interpersonal relationships
Advancement	Working conditions

To explain this, let's imagine that a person's level of motivation can exist on a scale that ranges from positive 10 to negative 10. If a person is at positive 10, they are extremely motivated. If a person is at zero, they are neither motivated nor demotivated (neutral). If a person is at negative 10, they are extremely demotivated.

Herzberg's theory suggests that if a person perceives that the motivating factors are present and/or regards them positively in their environment, then these factors are likely to contribute to that person's motivation score being positive. If these motivating factors are not present or are perceived negatively, they will contribute to the person's motivation score being neutral at worst.

On the other hand, Herzberg suggests that if any of the hygiene factors are in place and/or regarded positively by a person, then their contribution will at best be neutral to the person's motivation score. If these hygiene factors are not in place and/or perceived negatively, they will contribute to the person's motivation score being negative.

What I like about this theory is that by identifying motivating factors, it helps quantum leaders narrow down the options for increasing motivation and in turn increasing energy. In short, to increase energy, quantum leaders should focus on:

Achievement — Does the person feel challenged by their work and does it result in something meaningful?

Recognition — Does the person feel personally acknowledged for their efforts?

Nature of work — Does the type of work the person is doing suit their style?

Responsibility — Does the person feel trusted to deliver what they are being asked to deliver?

Advancement — Does the person see opportunities to progress their career, skills and experience as a result of their work?

I think it is also very interesting to understand that the factors that are listed as hygiene factors, according to Herzberg, have little positive contribution to motivation and can really only ever be de-motivators if they are either absent or perceived as lacking in some way. I have seen many organisations spend significant time and money on any number of these factors in the belief that they will act as strong motivators for staff when they can really only ever have a neutral impact on motivation at best.

There are many approaches that leaders can take that will likely have a positive impact on motivation by addressing one or more of the five motivating factors identified by Herzberg. I would like to focus on two strategies which I believe can motivate people very effectively.

Motivational and developmental delegation

In chapter 2, I have already discussed the importance of leaders being able to use different styles of delegation to be able to get more things done by other people than they might normally do. I discussed using directing, coaching, and deputising approaches to delegation as appropriate options which leaders can choose based on criteria such as the impact of the work, the priority of the work, the complexity of the work, and the degree of monitoring required based on the skill/experience/capacity of the person being delegated to.

These are all very important criteria, but they are all about the work itself and the current status of the person to whom the leader has decided to delegate the work. A quantum leader can also utilise Herzberg's motivational factors to add some further criteria to help better determine to whom the work should be delegated. The following questions should be considered:

1. Does this work represent a challenge to the person?

2. Does this work recognise the person in some way?

3. Does the style of this work suit the person?

4. Does the proposed delegation approach provide appropriate responsibility and/or authority to the person?

5. Does this work provide a development opportunity to the person that will help them advance?

My strong advice is that quantum leaders should not only ask themselves these questions to help decide who to delegate to, they should share these answers with the person they have selected.

These answers help leaders provide a compelling reason why they are delegating this work to that person and will give that person an immediate boost of motivation, even before the work has commenced.

As I discussed in chapter 2, in my experience, the majority of leaders involve themselves personally in the 'doing' of far too many things. It can be seen now that this becomes far more than just a problem of the leaders being stretched too thin and being unable to focus on the higher order requirements of their leadership role in any kind of quality way. It is also a major problem for the motivation and energy of the people they lead. Every task that leaders take on personally should be viewed as a potential missed opportunity to significantly motivate and energise someone else.

The three horizons of growth

One of the motivational factors that Herzberg identifies in his theory is that of the 'type of work'. This begs the question, 'What type of work will suit each person?' In chapter 2, I suggested that an understanding of an individual's strengths (via a tool like CliftonStrengths) and preferred operating styles (via a tool like our ECOS model) is absolutely critical for quantum leaders. Without doubt, understanding these things can also provide leaders with clues as to the type of work individuals are likely to be motivated (or demotivated) by.

I would like to suggest another way that quantum leaders can consider the 'type of work' question when it comes to motivation, and it revolves around a model that was introduced in a book titled, *The alchemy of growth*, written by three former McKinsey consultants, Mehrdad Baghai, Stephen Coley, and David White.

The fundamental premise of this book suggests that if organisations want to grow sustainably, they must consider and appropriately attend to three horizons of growth. I believe the three horizons concept provides leaders with a different lens through which to consider how people are motivated by the type of work they are doing. I will provide a very succinct summary of these three horizons and then focus on them through the lenses of motivation and type of work. I highly recommend the book to any leader as a compelling investigation of the nature of organisational growth and also as a very powerful approach to strategic planning.

Horizon 1

Horizon 1 represents current, well established business initiatives that an organisation is engaging in. These initiatives currently generate the bulk of the organisation's income/profit. They are well known and understood and tend to be relatively stable with few surprises. Horizon 1 is analogous to an Olympic rowing crew racing their boat across a flat lake. They are an efficient, well-balanced and stable team which strives to fine-tune its performance to get every ounce out of themselves and their boat. There are very few surprises — the lake is dead calm and they have done it hundreds of times before.

The alchemy of growth suggests that organisations can and should look to drive growth from this horizon by focusing on improving processes and practices, driving efficiency, fine-tuning, quality control and continuous improvement. The type of work that tends to occur in horizon 1 initiatives will therefore tend to motivate people who like stability, like to analyse things, do not mind repetition and refinement, are happy to work alone for extended periods of time, and who see small improvements as important achievements.

Horizon 2

Horizon 2 represents the new business initiatives that the organisation has decided to initiate. They are unlikely to be generating much profit for the organisation yet, and most likely are still requiring investment. They are very new and very exciting and have a lot of potential. These initiatives tend to move very quickly and can change just as quickly. They are inherently unstable, and problems and surprises can and do occur regularly. Horizon 2 is analogous to white water rafting or shooting the rapids. It is fast, exhilarating, and full of action and adventure. At any moment, anything could happen — the raft could capsize, hit a rock, hit a standing wave, be thrown into the air, people could be thrown overboard, etc. Of course, those in the raft will also get a very exciting ride and probably an extreme adrenalin rush to go along with it. The possibilities are seemingly unlimited!

The alchemy of growth suggests that organisations need initiatives in this horizon to provide new growth, with the focus needing to be on turning the potential these initiatives offer into reality. This requires problem solving skills, a preparedness to take risks, creative thinking, and a strong action-orientation. The type of work that is required in horizon 2 initiatives will therefore tend to motivate people who enjoy a challenge, love excitement and opportunity, like to make things happen, and crave variety.

Horizon 3

Horizon 3 represents the business initiatives that the organisation has identified as being future possibilities and worthy of further investigation. They are not just a wish list of possibilities, they are initiatives for which proper due diligence is being completed to ensure there is enough evidence to suggest that they are a real possibility. Importantly, the organisation has not yet decided to hit the 'go' button fully but is very interested in these initiatives. They are quite likely creative initiatives that have the opportunity to take the organisation to places it has not yet been. Horizon 3 is like scuba diving on the Great Barrier Reef. It is a world full of colour, wonder and endless possibility. It is a real world, but very different from the world we live in on the land. In this world, anything can come into view and should be viewed in all its wonder before moving on. It is also a world that requires preparation, knowledge, experience and a sense of caution to ensure we do not 'touch' the wrong things!

The alchemy of growth suggests that organisations need initiatives in this horizon in order to provide a future pipeline of growth opportunities. This horizon can require a wide range of skills ranging from creativity and envisioning skills at one end of the spectrum to business modelling, forecasting and research skills at the other. The type of work that is required in horizon 3 initiatives can be very motivational to a range of different people. In this horizon, teams with a diverse range of skills and strengths are required.

Implications for motivation

If quantum leaders consider the current business initiatives underway in their organisations and categorise them using the three horizons model, it is likely that many potential opportunities to better motivate people will present themselves. As a minimum, it is highly instructive to categorise each initiative into one of the horizons and then look at the people who are currently working on them to determine whether they fit the profile of someone who is likely to be motivated in that horizon. My experience has been that many people are working in horizons that they are unlikely to be motivated by. In these cases, they are like goldfish swimming in polluted fish bowls! 'Changing the water' of these people's 'goldfish bowls' might provide a significant increase in motivation and energy levels.

It is also likely to become apparent when initiatives are categorised in this way that there is an abundance of opportunity to move people around into different initiatives, which are likely to better match their 'type of work' motivational profile. At any one time, most large organisations have a plethora of projects going on over and above 'business as usual'. Each of these should be viewed as a motivational opportunity. Apart from the 'type of work' factor, they may also play to the other motivational factors (i.e. responsibility, achievement, recognition, advancement) for certain people as well.

Morale

I believe that most people do not need too much convincing when I say that a high level of morale generally equates to a higher level of energy, be that in an individual, in a team, or across an entire organisation. To be able to determine what they can do to encourage high levels of morale, quantum leaders should understand what really drives higher levels of morale in these entities.

My *Macquarie Dictionary* defines morale as 'a moral or mental condition with respect to cheerfulness, confidence and zeal'. Google's dictionary defines it as 'the confidence, enthusiasm and discipline of a person or group at a particular time'. The *Cambridge English Dictionary* provides two definitions, the first being 'the amount of confidence felt by a person or group of people, particularly in a dangerous or difficult situation'; the second, 'the level of satisfaction felt by a person or group of people who work together'.

When I extract the six key words from each of these definitions — confidence, cheerfulness, satisfaction, discipline, enthusiasm and zeal — I see the first three as being ingredients for creating energy, and the last three as being evidence that energy has been generated. Another way of saying this is that the first three words are inputs and the last three are outputs.

I am going to focus mainly on leadership strategies that can help increase the 'input' factors listed above. But before I do that, let me point out why each of the output factors are such strong evidence that energy has been generated.

When we consider a person who is said to have good discipline, there is a very strong implication that this person is taking the harder of two options. Taking the harder option requires more energy. I think about the discipline required to exercise regularly as an example. It takes no discipline at all to hit the snooze button, roll over and go back to sleep instead of getting up and going to the gym. It might well be easier not to make the effort, but we all know the long-term health effects of exercise if we just do it. The same can be said of just about any positive leadership skill or behaviour. It takes a lot of discipline (and energy) to make the effort to put them into practice and it is far easier not to bother, but we all know the long-term business benefits of positive leadership practices if we make the effort and just do them!

People who are enthusiastic seem to be bubbling over with energy. These are the people who volunteer, who go above and beyond, who do not get discouraged when problems occur, and who happily pitch in and help others who need it. They are also the people whose own enthusiasm can rub off on others. All of these things require a lot of energy.

To my way of thinking, zeal is almost a combination of discipline and enthusiasm — we could call it disciplined enthusiasm. *The Macquarie Dictionary* describes it as 'ardour for a person, cause or object' and 'eager desire or endeavour'. In short, zealots (people with zeal) are going to fight enthusiastically for a cause and have the discipline to sustain the fight until victory has been achieved, even if the fight is difficult or dangerous.

I do not know about you, but I think any organisation populated with disciplined, enthusiastic zealots for the cause of the organisation is going to be something of an irresistible force. All of these attributes are outcomes of high morale. I think it is therefore fair to say that morale is anything but a 'soft', 'nice to have' in an organisation. It is a game-changing *must* have!

Let's now focus on the 'inputs' to morale — confidence, cheerfulness, and satisfaction. We have already covered each of these to some degree in chapter 4, which focuses on the trust factor of the quantum equation. We saw then that confidence, joy (cheerfulness/fun), and satisfaction are all increased when the various waves of trust (particularly self-trust, relationship trust, and organisational trust) are in place. But apart from following the suggestions I made to build trust at all of these levels, what else can quantum leaders focus on to really build energy through confidence, cheerfulness, and satisfaction?

I am going to share some practical examples from my own corporate experience at Compaq Computer Australia in the 1990s. I am using this example because I witnessed first-hand how the company created a very high level of confidence, cheerfulness and satisfaction (i.e. a very high morale) through activities and rituals that were nothing to do specifically with the work that people were doing. The first example I would like to highlight is the power of a strong and vibrant social club.

My wife, Suzanne, joined Compaq in 1991 soon after we were married, and she moved from our home city of Brisbane to join me in Sydney (where I had moved two years earlier after graduating from university). This meant she was moving to a new job in a new company in a new city, where she pretty much only knew one person — me!

It turned out that while Compaq was still only a small company in Australia (it had about fifty staff), it had a very enthusiastic social committee that was charged with organising regular social events of various kinds for staff, their partners and families. Within a few weeks of Suzanne starting at Compaq, we were attending our first social club event, a novelty trivia night! This event was hilarious and hugely enjoyable and fun. The novelty component of the evening involved earning bonus points for activities like joke-telling, bubble (gum) blowing, impromptu speeches, celebrity impressions, etc. What I also really liked about the event was that pretty much everyone in the company attended, including the CEO and all of the senior executives, and the partners (no children at this particular event) of every staff member were made to feel just as welcome as all of the staff. In fact, by the end of that night, I felt like I had made a number of really good friends already myself. We all partied hard that night, laughed our heads off, and loved every minute of it. (I think our team might have even won the entire event — though that part is now a bit blurry!)

It was only a few weeks later that we were attending our next social club event, the annual Compaq tennis day. This was again an extremely fun day, with partners and families (kids allowed this time) welcomed to participate fully. If you did not get to meet someone on the tennis court, you certainly got to meet them at the barbecue, or sitting around having a picnic, or having a drink at the bar. A few weeks later it was a beach volleyball tournament and family picnic day. I think you are probably getting the picture. The events just kept on coming!

After a few months of this, not only had Suzanne made a lot of friends in Compaq, she felt like she truly belonged. The fascinating thing was, so did I! Even though I did not actually work for the company, I really felt like I was a part of it and had a lot of affection for it. When I received a call from the HR director of Compaq in early 1993 suggesting that there was a job in their sales department that I might want to consider applying for, I did not hesitate! Even though I had loved working for my previous company, Honeywell, for the past three years, I knew there was something special about Compaq and I really wanted to be part of it.

For the nearly 10 years that I worked for Compaq, the social club remained a huge part of the organisation's DNA. Even when the company grew to be thousands of people, we went out of our way to keep the social club activities rolling out regularly, to give staff and their families a sense of belonging and the chance to build relationships across the organisation. The payback to the organisation of this was enormous. Compaq became a place where no problem could not be fixed, where people would work all night to help out their colleagues if they needed help, and where every employee was a zealot for Compaq's products and its goal to become the number one PC company in the world. Unsurprisingly, we achieved our goal of knocking IBM off the number one perch in 1997 and stayed there until the company merged with HP shortly after I left the organisation in 2001.

Twenty years on, in a world that continues to throw up challenge after challenge, change after change, I believe quantum leaders could learn a few lessons from the way Compaq did things in the 1990s, and realise that investing time, effort and money into developing a vibrant and active social club and actively participating in these events is an extremely effective way to build confidence, cheerfulness and satisfaction.

One final and simple suggestion I have for increasing the 'input' factor of morale is the practice of MBWA — management by walking around!

Compaq's CEO from the company's foundation in Australia in 1985 until his retirement in 2000 was a gentleman by the name of Ian Penman. Ian's success and endurance in a CEO role in the IT industry of the 80s and 90s is a testament to his leadership abilities. In fact, Ian used to proudly say that in his time at Compaq he had outlasted 11 CEOs of IBM. So it is fair to say that Ian was, and still is, a legend in the Australian IT industry.

One habit of Ian's was that he practised MBWA regularly. He took the time to go for a walk around the floors of our office building, or down to the distribution and service centre. He did not make a big deal of it, he just quietly wandered around. But what he always did was take the time to pop his head in to say hello to random people along the way. He did this in a very friendly and non-threatening way and with no fixed agenda. He asked people how they were personally, how their work was going, and whether there was anything he could do to help them out. Every person he spoke to felt that he cared about them personally, that he knew and was interested in what they were doing, and that they were an important part of the overall organisation.

Suzanne was Ian's personal assistant for her first couple of years with Compaq, so I can tell you that Ian was just as busy as any CEO I have ever worked with. His diary could look like a nightmare at times. But he always made his MBWA a priority and did not let other more 'urgent' matters distract him from this important ritual. To my way of thinking, doing MBWA every now and then is nice, but doing it regularly is a game changer for the confidence, cheerfulness and satisfaction of people all over any organisation.

Meaning

I have already discussed the very strong link between societal trust and energy in chapter 4. In short, I suggested that people are highly energised if they have a strong belief in the purpose or meaning of their work. It is critical that quantum leaders emphasise the community and societal impacts that their organisations are having and ensure the people of the organisation are fully aware of their contribution to these impacts.

Let me give you a specific example from my time as director of the Consumer Division at Compaq Computer Australia. For several years in the mid-1990s, our division grew at an extremely rapid pace, riding on the back of the home PC boom and the early days of the internet. At the height of this boom, our consumer sales grew at 50 to 100 per cent per year for four years in a row. Our biggest problem was often that we could not get enough computers to keep up with the demand from our retail partners. It was an exciting time, we had a lot of fun, but everyone also worked long and hard hours to try to keep up with the growth.

One day, out of nowhere, a lady by the name of Nicole Bosland, our national sales manager for the Consumer Division, came to me and said that she was feeling really tired, de-energised and a bit disheartened.

This came as a shock to me. This lady was an absolute star performer. She was killing her sales targets, leading a great sales team, and had great career prospects within Compaq. She also happened to be a national champion in Latin-American ballroom dancing. Clearly, she was an incredibly driven, talented, and disciplined person. Yet, here she was saying that she was de-energised and disheartened.

When I asked her a few more questions about what was going on, she eventually said to me that she did not really know why we were doing what we were doing. It seemed to her that we were selling and shipping out thousands and thousands of boxes, day after day, month after month, year after year, and all that she could see coming down the track was more and more of the same. Every year the organisation would expect higher sales, the retailers would expect more product at better margins, competitors would continue to make life harder and harder, and she would have to ask her team to do more and more while becoming ever more efficient. It really was all sounding rather grim.

When I look back on what I did next, I would love to say that it was because I was such a great leader or a great coach, but in truth, it was because I needed to rush off to another meeting! I suggested that we both go away overnight and try to think of an answer to 'Why are we doing this?' I then suggested that we reconvene the next day to share what we had each come up with.

When I stopped and considered the question myself, my first answer was actually, 'To keep the vice-president in Singapore happy and not roasting my backside for missing my forecast numbers!' I realised this was not a great answer and that my own energy levels were getting pretty depleted, and I had lost some of the excitement and joy I had felt about Compaq in my earlier years. Clearly, I also needed to think about this question much more deeply.

When we met again the next day, both of us had given the question considerable thought. Interestingly, we had both come up with answers that had a lot of similarities. We both felt that by making computers a reality in the homes of so many Australians, we were helping to empower every Australian family with access to information and knowledge far in excess of anything that had ever existed in history. We realised that we were helping to improve the education of children, we were connecting families, and we were entertaining people. All of this had nothing to do with the short-term sales numbers that we were both on the line for.

Unsurprisingly, after this conversation, our star national sales manager was off and running again with renewed energy and purpose, and continued on her very successful path, going far above what was expected on many occasions. My own energy was also recharged, and I went on to have some courageous discussions about the topic of our 'real' purpose with that same vice-president in Singapore. I suggested that maybe we needed to make it more about our contribution to society and not just about this month's numbers. As a product guy who had come out of our factory in Houston and basically never spoken to a customer or end-user in his life, I am not sure that my version of the 'real' purpose made any sense to him, but me 'talking straight' with him about some of the less than ideal interactions we had been having certainly moved our relationship in the right direction from that point.

While the example I have provided above is talking about building energy at an individual level, the exact same principle applies at a team and overall organisational level. The more people feel aligned with and believe in the purpose they are working towards, the greater the energy levels will be in the team or organisation. Ensuring that members of any team or organisation have a clear and agreed purpose for their work, and that they believe in the contribution of that purpose to the greater good, is a vital step for quantum leaders to take.

Modelling

As I have already stated, human beings build energy in many ways, some of them physiological, some of them psychological. What this really means is that the physical and mental health of an individual has a lot to do with the amount of energy they have available to use. The other '3Ms' of energy all tend to be talking about things that a quantum leader can do to positively impact on the psychological state of people to, in turn, build their energy. Modelling is all about the physiological state of people.

Unfortunately, no person can force another person to be physically healthy. Physical health is largely the result of decisions that individuals make for themselves. What quantum leaders can do is model a healthy lifestyle and healthy decisions through their own behaviours. This is a true case of 'leading by example'.

Many years ago, there was a television advertisement in Australia that said something like 'Everywhere you go, everything you do, someone is watching you!' It was targeted at parents who drank and smoked and suggested that their children were watching and learning their habits from them all of the time. Very true in my experience! Well, it is also very true for organisational leaders. People look to leaders to see how they behave and to determine what is acceptable. They will often be very strongly influenced by the habits and behaviours of a leader, particularly a leader who is someone they look up to or aspire to be like. So, if quantum leaders want people to be energetic, one of the best things they can do is model a healthy lifestyle that builds energy.

I am not a wellness or health expert, but here are a few tips I have picked up along the way that can really help build a leader's own energy and simultaneously demonstrate good practices and behaviours to others.

Control stress

Stress-induced emotions consume a huge amount of energy. Stress will usually be brought on by the perception of some kind of imminent threat in the immediate environment. In my experience, in the organisational context there are two types of threat that leaders can get stressed about: 1. Threats created by other people — a boss, a customer, a colleague, a staff member, 2. Self-created threats. It has also been my experience that many perceived threats can be significantly over-exaggerated.

The first thing I suggest if leaders are feeling stressed is that they need to take the time to identify what they think the threat is and which of the above two categories it fits into. If the threat fits into category 1, they need to identify who the other party is and then go and discuss the perceived threat with that person. More often than not, if leaders are prepared to share that they perceive a threat, the discussion will clarify things and remove the stress completely. If the threat fits into category 2, they need to take a realistic look at the situation and reset their own expectations to reduce the stress created. So many times statements like, 'I must get this done by ...' or 'I must ensure this is perfect' are not helpful and not necessary, yet they can become habit and produce stress when there is no real reason for it.

Stress is definitely something that a leader can make other people experience. If the leader is stressed, everyone around the leader is likely to become stressed. As I have mentioned previously, stress increases the amount of the chemical cortisol in the body. This chemical is part of the 'flight or fight' response of the body and is designed to protect us from immediate threat. It has the effect of sending energy to the major muscle groups of the body to enable us to take action (either flight or fight) in a short burst. The problem is that all of this energy is taken from other parts of the body, like the frontal cortex of the brain, which is responsible for creativity, problem solving, regulation of emotion and many other 'higher order' functions.

I have discussed in detail the importance of things like creativity, innovation, and emotional intelligence in other parts of this book. If leaders are stressed and are stressing everyone else around them, it is basically a chemical impossibility to draw these functions from either themselves or those other people.

Reducing stress can be achieved in many ways including talking to friends or relatives, working with an executive coach, joining a support group, or seeking therapeutic help in extreme cases. Relaxation therapies like massage, meditation, yoga, and tai chi can be terrific stress relievers as can engaging in some form of sport or exercise. Demonstrating the opposite of stress (i.e. calmness, steadiness, control), particularly in anything resembling a 'crisis', is one of the best ways that quantum leaders can model healthy behaviour to their people and generate significantly better outcomes.

Do less, achieve more

According to a recent article I read from *Harvard Health Publishing*, one of the main reasons people feel fatigued is overwork. Overwork is essentially people trying to pack every available moment of their lives with activity, be it professional, family or social obligations. Many executives with whom I have worked over the years describe their lives as being analogous to a hamster running on a wheel. Is it any wonder people operating this way never seem to have enough energy to perform at their optimal levels?

We have all heard the saying 'work smarter not harder'. In my opinion, in the quantum environments in which most leaders are operating these days, if they are not working smart, they are failing. What do I mean by working smart? I mean focusing on quality rather than quantity. All of the techniques, ideas, and behaviours I have outlined in this book for quantum leaders are not 'quantity' tasks, they are 'quality' strategies. They require thought and planning, not knee-jerk reaction.

In chapter 2, I explained that implementing appropriate priority management strategies for themselves, their teams and their organisations is a critical skill for quantum leaders. In the context of this topic, these priority management strategies can be a critical energy builder. All tasks, whether they are important or not, take energy to complete. Quantum leaders need to ensure they are investing their energy in important activities that have a high impact on their organisations and not wasting their energy on unimportant tasks. This means learning to politely say 'no' when asked to get involved in things that are not important in the big scheme of things. It means delegating effectively to ensure the abilities and resources of other people are being properly leveraged. It also means ensuring enough time is allowed to do a quality job of the important tasks that leaders decide to complete themselves.

Modelling by quantum leaders of good prioritisation and appropriate investment of energy is something that sets the tone for staff and leaders right throughout an organisation.

Exercise

While I am not an expert on exercise physiology, I do absolutely know, as I am sure most people do, that exercise gives the human body's cells more energy to burn through more efficient operation of the digestive system (nutrition), the respiratory system (breathing), and the circulatory system (heart function and blood flow). If all of these systems are functioning optimally, the body is able to extract the full energy value from the food we eat and the oxygen we breathe and circulate this energy efficiently and effectively to all parts of our bodies. It is also highly likely people who exercise regularly are likely to get more and better-quality sleep. (I will have more to say about sleep shortly.)

Our bodies also produce tiny neurochemicals called endorphins when we exercise. The basic function of endorphins is to act as a natural pain reliever and enhance pleasure. By promoting an overall sense of wellbeing, endorphins have many benefits including alleviating depression, reducing stress and anxiety, and boosting self-esteem.

Clearly, there are obvious physical benefits to exercise as well. Unfortunately, many roles in modern organisations are quite sedentary in nature. As such, it is not uncommon to see senior executives who have neglected their physical wellbeing through poor diet and lack of exercise, and who, as a result, look anything but healthy. When leaders consider their personal brand image and the impression this gives other people, walking around looking like a 'heart attack waiting to happen' is hardly inspiring! On the other hand, leaders modelling good health and self-care can have a massive flow on benefit in their organisations.

Avoid obviously unhealthy habits

I do not want to preach to you about the topics that are grouped under this heading. Obviously, avoiding smoking, excessive alcohol intake, excessive caffeine intake, and excessive sugar intake are all well documented ways of improving health and wellbeing. What is also interesting, though, is how these are all potential sources of significant energy depletion.

Smoking significantly depletes energy by causing insomnia. The nicotine in tobacco is a stimulant, so it speeds up the heart rate, raises blood pressure, stimulates the brain-wave activity associated with alertness and wakefulness, and therefore makes it hard to go to sleep. It is also quite likely that once a smoker does fall asleep, the addictive power of nicotine can wake them up again in order to indulge the craving. This lack of quality, energy replenishing sleep can be a major issue.

Alcohol can significantly reduce energy because it has a sedative effect. Typically, within an hour of drinking alcohol, some form of sedating effect will be felt by the drinker. Drinking at lunch time is likely to produce some form of mid-afternoon slump and drinking at dinner time is likely to produce a sense of tiredness or drowsiness into the evening. Alcohol is also a depressant and can have a blunting effect on many mental functions, so it is not a particularly useful contributor to most activities that are typically expected of effective leaders.

Caffeine is another form of stimulant which can produce short term increases in alertness, but when overused can cause higher levels of anxiety, heart palpitations, increased brain-wave activity, and, of course, insomnia or interrupted sleep. Judiciously choosing when to enjoy a coffee to ensure the negative energy effects do not accumulate is a very worthwhile practice for leaders.

One common effect that all of the above habits share, along with the use of many illicit drugs, is that they all increase the level of a neurotransmitter in the brain called dopamine. Dopamine is a very important chemical which relays signals around the brain. It is produced in two areas of the brain, with the dopamine from one area associated with many aspects of movement and speech (Parkinson's disease is associated with a lack of dopamine from this area of the brain), and dopamine from the other areas associated with reward and reinforcement. It is the reward and reinforcement function of dopamine that can cause problems if it gets out of balance.

The 'high' that people get from any form of drug (or anything else that makes them feel good) is caused by the increased levels of dopamine generated in the brain (basically reinforcing the good feeling associated with the experience). What people get addicted to is actually the dopamine hit and even though they know the thing that produced the hit is bad for them, they keep going back for more. Unfortunately, over time, people need to take more of a drug to produce the same dopamine high, which means their addiction can spiral out of control.

Eat smart

From an energy perspective, each individual has their own metabolism. That is, we all digest and process foods and nutrients at different speeds, and we all require varying levels of fats, proteins, carbohydrates, and nutrients. For some people, it is definitely better to eat small meals and healthy snacks every few hours as opposed to having three large meals a day. Yet other people do really well practising something like intermittent fasting, whereby they are confining their food consumption to an 8-hour window each day. Both approaches, and others, can provide the body with the nutrients it requires, providing we really adhere to the principle of eating high quality food.

Eating food with a low glycaemic index (sugars that are digested slowly) will help avoid the big energy decline that typically occurs after eating food with quickly absorbed sugars or refined starches (e.g. lollies/candy, chocolate, potato chips). Low glycaemic index foods include high-fibre vegetables, nuts, and healthy oils (e.g. olive oil, coconut oil). In general, high carbohydrate foods have the highest glycaemic index. Grains are tricky in today's world, and our bodies will generally do better without them. Similarly, gluten-free breads have a higher glycaemic index than normal bread. Artificial sweeteners are never healthy. These changes can seem overwhelming, but they are attainable with good advice and good planning.

Drink more water

Most people are actually existing in varying states of dehydration. When the body does not have enough water, one of the first signs is a loss of energy and a feeling of fatigue. Water has been shown to enhance performance for all but the most demanding endurance sports, so for typical leaders in typical organisational environments, it will more than meet their needs.

Many people do not realise that water is continually depleting from their bodies when they sit in air-conditioned environments, when they speak in meetings, and, when they move anywhere throughout the day. Dehydration also contributes to insomnia or sleep interruption which, as we have already discussed, interferes with the replenishment of energy that we all need.

I was told by a nutrition consultant at my gym that for every 40 kg of body weight, a person should be drinking at least one litre of water to replenish what they are losing each day. When I heard that, I realised that I was way short of that mark on my water intake.

Quantity and quality of sleep

Having considered the preceding topics, it is clear that negatively affected sleep is a sure-fire way to reduce energy. Everybody needs sleep and everybody is negatively affected by a lack of it, or a lack of quality sleep. Just about every type of tissue and system in the body — including the brain, heart, lungs, metabolism, immune function, emotions, and disease resistance — is affected by the quantity and quality of sleep a person gets. A lack of quality sleep has been proven to contribute to high blood pressure, cardiovascular disease, depression, diabetes and obesity. So, in short, when we consider it from a physiological perspective, getting more quality sleep is a no brainer!

There is a lot of advice around about how we can give ourselves a better chance of getting good quality sleep. We have already discussed eating and drinking habits, exercise, hydration, etc. I think the suggestion to 'disconnect' ourselves from our various devices and/ or reducing screen time for at least 30 minutes to an hour before going to bed is of particular relevance. The stimulation to our brains and the thought activation that happens when we are 'connected' is a recipe for lack of, or poor quality, sleep.

One very strong link to the issue of stress is the habit that many leaders have of working late at night (or into the early hours of the morning) and continuing to send emails to their staff and/or other people in the organisation at those hours. Not only does this increase the stress and reduce the sleep of the leader, it also creates huge stress on and affects the quality of sleep of everyone around that leader. There is nothing worse than going to bed worrying about what urgent email from your boss might be waiting for you when you wake up. This creates a feeling of constant 'threat' and as such increases the stress levels (and levels of cortisol) in everyone operating in that environment.

So, regardless of which of the above health-related behaviours a quantum leader models, many people will take their cue from this modelling. People may not do everything exactly the same as the leader, but even if they mimic just one of these positive behaviours, there will likely be a valuable energy dividend.

Quantum leaders — you've got this!

While I have covered a large number of topics and provided many ideas in this book, I really want readers to remember that, at its core, quantum leadership is quite a simple concept and is something that can be applied in a pragmatic way to any individual, team or organisation.

All a leader needs to do to excite a quantum leap in the performance of any entity is to find one way to increase each of the capability, trust and energy factors for that particular entity and execute these simultaneously. The increases can be small, but if they happen together, the impact will be huge.

Leaders should have the quantum equation burned in their memories: $Q = C \times T^2 \times E^2$

To conclude, I have provided below a high-level summary of the options I have suggested for increasing each of the quantum equation factors for individuals, teams and organisations. For any situation, choose one option for each factor and develop a strategy to implement it. If an option does not work immediately, do not give up on it. Use the Reflect, Plan, Act cycle to refine your approach and try it again. If that does not work, try a different option.

One final suggestion is to use your own knowledge and experience to add to the strategies I have outlined. Do not be afraid to use this. If any of my suggestions remind you of things you already know or have experienced, that is terrific! Go for it, give those ideas a try. A true quantum leap in performance is closer than you realise.

Increasing the quantum equation factors

Individuals	Increasing capability	Utilise a coaching discovery methodology **(Happy–Sad–Happy)** to identify capabilities and development needs.
		Complete a **Clifton Strengthsfinder** assessment to identify individual talents and strengths.
		Complete a **360-degree capability assessment** (e.g. Executive Central's LCAT) to identify capabilities and development needs.
		Utilise an accelerated **Reflect, Plan, Act cycle** to develop solutions and refine those solutions to identified capability development needs.
		Utilise the **motivational and developmental delegation model** to expose individuals to new challenges and to build new skills.
	Increasing trust	Use the **four cores of credibility** to identify where you could build more trust with the individual and how they could build trust with others.
		Use the **13 trust-building behaviours** to identify where you could build more trust with the individual and how they could build trust with others.
		Analyse your relationship with the individual using the **four types of stakeholder relationship model** and develop actions to elevate it to a higher level.
		Ask yourself the **'leader trust' questions** with respect to that individual.
	Increasing energy	Ask the **five motivational factor questions** with respect to the individual.
		Consider the individual's level of morale and find more opportunities for them to feel a sense of belonging.

Individuals	Increasing energy	Consider the degree to which the individual connects with the meaning of their work.
		Consider what level of energy, health and wellbeing you are modelling to that individual.
		Utilise the **motivational and developmental delegation model** to provide the individual with new and challenging tasks and development opportunities.
		Consider the **three horizons of growth model** to determine which horizon is most likely to motivate the individual.
		Identify opportunities that will allow the individual to utilise strengths and capabilities that they already have but are underutilising.
		Coach the individual to flex their operating style to demonstrate stronger emotional intelligence and create a more comfortable work environment with others.
		Flex your own operating style to create a more comfortable working environment with the individual.
Teams	Increasing capability	Assess the team against the **five drivers of superior teams** and act to address any shortfalls in these team capabilities.
		Introduce the **quantum team structure**, led by a deep understanding of the strengths of each team member and cross-team accountability.
		Coach each team member to delegate and prioritise more effectively to make more time for cross-team accountabilities.
		Flex your own operating style to more effectively take advantage of the diversity of styles within the team.
		Coach team members to flex their operating styles more effectively when working within the team.

Teams	Increasing trust	Consider the extent to which the **four cores of credibility** are evident within the team.
		Consider the extent to which the **13 trust-building behaviours** are being demonstrated within the team.
		Consider the quality of interpersonal relationships between team members against the **four types of stakeholder relationship model**.
		Demonstrate vulnerability yourself within the team to show that it is safe to do so (e.g. discuss mistakes openly, challenge constructively).
	Increasing energy	Consider the degree to which motivational factors are in place and positively regarded within the team.
		Encourage regular team building and social activities to increase team morale.
		Ensure the team has a clear and agreed purpose and team members individually connect to the importance of this purpose.
		Consider the energy you are displaying to the team (e.g. the degree of stress you display, the health and wellbeing you display).
		Openly reward and recognise examples of team members expending their own energy to help other team members.
Organisations	Increasing capability	Conduct the **change audit process** to review changes that have impacted the organisation in the past 12 months and assess the degree of innovation demonstrated in response.
		Conduct an **OIE assessment** to identify innovation related capabilities throughout the organisation.
		Introduce development in support of the **4Cs associated with innovation**.

Organisations	Increasing trust	Assess/scan the organisational ecosystem (policies, procedures) to identify where trust has been eroded and work with those affected to fix these issues.
		Answer the **market/societal trust questions** with respect to the organisation.
		Assess the extent to which people align with and understand the organisation's overarching purpose.
		Assess the extent to which you and leaders at all levels of the organisation behave consistently with the stated organisational values.
	Increasing energy	Ensure reward and recognition policies within the organisation effectively address both **motivational and hygiene factors**.
		Introduce and/or actively participate in the organisation's social club and ensure partners and families of staff are welcomed to participate.
		Consider the degree to which the organisation contributes to society (e.g. worthwhile charities) and how involved staff are in these initiatives.
		Consider the energy that you and leaders at all levels of the organisation are modelling through your health and wellbeing practices.

Further reading

Anderson, M & Jefferson, M, 2018, *Transforming organizations: engaging the 4Cs for powerful organizational learning and change*, Bloomsbury Business, Sydney.

Baghai, M, Coley, S & White, D, 1999, *The alchemy of growth: kickstarting and sustaining growth in your company*, Orion Business Books, London, UK.

Bass, BM & Riggio, RE, 2006, *Transformational leadership*, NJL Erlbaum Associates, Mahwah.

Collins, JC, 2001, *Good to great: why some companies make the leap and others don't*, HarperBusiness, New York.

Covey, SR & Covey, S, 2020, *The 7 habits of highly effective people*, Simon & Schuster, New York.

Covey, SR & Merrill, RR, 2006, *The speed of trust: the one thing that changes everything*, Simon & Schuster, New York.

Downes, L, 2009, *The laws of disruption: harnessing the new forces that govern life and business in the digital age*, Basic Books, New York.

Freiberg, K & Freiberg, J, 1998, *Nuts! Southwest Airlines' crazy recipe for business and personal success*, Crown Business, New York.

Goleman, D, 2006, *Emotional intelligence*, Bantam, London, UK

Henry, T, 2015, *Louder than words: harness the power of your authentic voice*, Penguin, New York.

Herzberg, F, 2005, 'Motivation-hygiene theory' in Miner, J, *Organisational behaviour I: essential theories of motivation and leadership*, pp. 61–74.

Lancaster, S, Di Milia, L & Cameron, R, 2013, 'Supervisor behaviours that facilitate training transfer', *Journal of Workplace Learning*, vol. 25, pp. 6–22.

Maslow, A & Lewis, K, 1987, 'Maslow's hierarchy of needs', Salenger Incorporated, vol. 14, p. 987.

McChrystal, GS, Collins, T, Silverman, D & Fussell, C, 2015, *Team of teams: new rules of engagement for a complex world*, Penguin, New York.

Sesno, F, 2017, *Ask more: the power of questions to open doors, uncover solutions, and spark change*, Amacom, New York.

Stephenson, P, 2002, *The naked executive: confronting the truth about leadership*, Pearson Education, Sydney, Australia.

Yaeger, D, 2016, *Great teams: 16 things high performing organisations do differently*, Thomas Nelson, Nashville.

Acknowledgments

No project of this kind is ever the work of just one person. I am extremely privileged to have been surrounded by people in both my personal and professional lives who have made it possible for me to write this book. I would like to acknowledge just how important they are to me.

My beautiful wife Suzanne, the best partner and friend anyone could ever hope for, has been a part of the Executive Central journey from day one, and has allowed me to pursue my business passions every step of the way. Without her behind-the-scenes efforts in running all aspects of the finance and operations of the company, we would not be in such an exciting phase of our operations. Suzanne, I love you very much and cannot wait to continue our life's journey together.

My wonderful children, Robbie, Stephanie and Ashleigh, inspire me with their adventures, passions, talents, and enthusiasm for life. Being their dad is the greatest thing I will ever do, and I love every minute of it. I cannot wait to see what the future has in store for each of them.

My mum and dad deserve all the credit for creating a family where my brother, sisters and I were encouraged and loved. I am fortunate to have an extended family where each of us really does like each other and thoroughly enjoys each other's company! Mum and Dad, I cannot thank you enough and I love you lots. I look forward to many more great family adventures in the future.

My great friends and wonderful business partners at Executive Central, Glenn and Reyna, are like my brother and sister. Their talents, knowledge and experience have played a significant part in the development of many of the concepts I have shared in this book. I am so proud of what we have built together at Executive Central and cannot wait to unlock its full potential in the coming years. Thank you.

Our newly appointed managing director at Executive Central, Todd Everitt, has made an unbelievable difference to our business, and his stewardship of the company through the difficult Covid-19 restriction period has been extraordinary. He has truly earned the trust and respect of the entire Executive Central team. My comfort in knowing the business is in such good hands has enabled me to significantly accelerate the completion of this book, for which I am truly grateful.

My coaching colleagues at Executive Central have contributed ideas and editing to this book, and I am grateful for their time and effort. I feel very privileged to work with such a talented group of executives. Thank you for your fellowship and collegiality, and for the contributions you have made over the years to the ever expanding pool of intellectual property we have developed as an organisation.

My former coach and employer, Peter Stephenson, started me off on my journey as an executive coach. It has been many years since we have spoken, but without the positive experience I had with him as my coach and the opportunity he gave me to run his company when I first left corporate life, I would never have taken this road. I learned a lot from him about leadership and running a professional services firm, and many of those lessons have had a major impact on the type of company I have built with my colleagues. All good wishes to you, Peter, and to Barbara.

Finally, it has truly been an honour and a privilege to work with many clients over the past twenty years as an executive coach and consultant. I consider myself incredibly lucky to be in a position where I am able to spend time with truly talented, enthusiastic, and interesting people, forming close friendships with many of them, and then to call that my job! In every assignment I have ever been involved in, I have learned at least as much from my clients as they have learned from me. Thank you for your support over the years and I really hope you enjoy this book, which is a culmination of all of that support.

Index